THE Grey Nomad's

ULTIMATE GUIDE TO AUSTRALIA

THE Grey Nomad's
ULTIMATE GUIDE TO AUSTRALIA

Experience the beauty and
freedom of our great landscape –
for young and old alike!

NEW HOLLAND

CONTENTS

FOREWORD

by Rob Catania of FRC (Full Range Camping)

If you are reading this, chances are you are about to embark on, or are planning to embark on, the adventure of a lifetime. Or perhaps you're already a somewhat seasoned adventurer and you want to know a little more. Maybe a *lot* more. Be it part-time, full-time or periodic, becoming a nomad can allow you to experience one of the greatest new adventures of your life. Be it grey, pink, green or otherwise, nomadding is colour-blind. It doesn't really matter how old you are either. The key word here is *nomad*.

And unless you have grown up in a family that did a lot of camping it might also mean a whole new way of life for you. Just as it was for us. In 2012, when we finally took the plunge, the nomad life was almost a complete mystery. So, there we were, my wife and I, with our small children and no knowledge of caravanning, and without ever even had a weekend camping trip. We embarked on what was and continues to be the best adventure of our lives.

It was a spur-of-the-moment decision, after being introduced to a family of nomads. They inspired us to spend the following twelve months redesigning our life and planning a trip around Australia. Packing the home and parking our business we set off to live full-time on the road in our motorhome with a six-year-old and a two-year-old. Yes, many would say we were crazy, and some people weren't even as flattering as that.

Our preparation at the time consisted of hours scouring the internet, not really knowing what to look for. We attended numerous caravan shows and spoke to as many people as we could about caravanning and camping. However, it was a long, drawn-out process, and finding all that we needed in one place was nearly impossible.

In hindsight, although we didn't realise it at the time, we probably headed off *slightly* unprepared, but for us that was part of the journey. As we got underway, we experienced adventure after adventure, from escaping bushfires to being airlifted from major floods. Along the way we have met and made incredible lifelong friends, and in the meantime have got to see the best this county has to offer.

However, learning as we went, allowed us to find there was something missing in the marketplace:

- A way to find thousands of campsites and RV related businesses easily
- A way to interact with other campers and nomads
- A way to research and buy an RV or camping gear, or sell it for that matter
- Somewhere to buy the latest camping products
- Somewhere to find new and exciting places to see
- A way to obtain discounts and save money while we travelled
- Somewhere that provided services specific to RVs and nomads such as RV insurance
- A way to put all that we have learnt and experienced into one place.

The list goes on and on, so with the assistance of our long-time friend Glen Wilson, we set about putting all this information in one place, and thus the FRC website and app were born: an all-in-one, one-stop shop for everything camping and caravanning.

That took a lot of time. In fact, it took over six years of development to amass the huge amount of information necessary for FRC to be a truly useful and comprehensive resource for campers and nomads in Australia. But there was *still* something missing. What we didn't have at the time of preparing for our trip was exactly what Xavier Waterkeyn has masterfully put together in this book.

This is a compendium or 'how-to' book to help you be better prepared and to give you the best possible introduction to the

nomadding life; a guide that tells you what to look out for and how to prepare, and then if you need further information where to find it. A manual that introduces you to the power of online resources that even people who are initially intimidated by technology will find easy to use, as well as an offline resource that you can access all the time, even when technology fails.

Carefully researched and written in a down-to-earth manner you will find this book a great asset in preparation for what you are about to embark on, whether it's your first step or your hundredth. It is something we wish we had read before preparing for our trip as it would have saved us *considerable* time, money and effort, both in the pre-planning stages, and while on the road.

We humbly thank Xavier and the whole team at New Holland for consulting us in his preparation of this book and allowing us to contribute with our experiences where possible. We hope you enjoy reading it, and that it will greatly benefit you in your preparations.

However, just remember, as prepared as you think you can be, the real fun is in the impromptu experience, there is no doubt, anything can and probably will happen, things that are not even in the scope of this book, but if they do, *embrace them and enjoy.*

All the best and happy camping!

Rob Catania
Co-Founder, FRC

INTRODUCTION

WHAT THIS BOOK WILL DO FOR YOU

Lots of people don't read introductions to books, and who can blame them? After all, there's a lot to be said to just jumping straight into a subject and getting on with it. But if you're reading this, let's use this introduction to give you some context for this book and how it will be useful to you.

The Grey Nomad's Ultimate Guide to Australia was written *specifically* with the grey nomad in mind. However, it has lots of useful information for campers of all colours and for holiday campers too.

This book was also written with the invaluable input of FRC, a company specifically created to provide services and resources to the camping and nomadding community and that's constantly developing an ever-wider network of contacts and building a community that all campers and nomads can access. They provided a lot of links for further reading and you'll find these scattered throughout the book, along with a few traveller's tales and illustrative anecdotes from FRC's Co-Director, Rob Catania. FRC also provided invaluable insider information about what nomadding is actually like – the sort of hard-earned information that only years of experience can give you – as well as insights into the sorts of challenges nomads face and the wealth of opportunities for fun and adventure that are available to nomads that their more settled brothers and sisters can only dream of.

In fact, it's the dream that gets nomads started on the life in the first place, and in this book we wanted to empower you as much as possible to live the dream. It's a dream that tens of thousands of Australians are living full time, and over a million a year are living part-time.

Even seasoned nomads don't know everything. Many will attest that they are constantly learning. We saw the need for an introduction to nomadding that would be useful both to those who are still in the dreaming stage and those who wanted to know more. We've come up with a great introduction to nomadding and this book will be a resource that you'll come back to again and again on your travels.

But no introductory book, no matter how well-researched or clearly written, can possibly tackle the *huge* subject of nomadding all on its own —with over 9000 campsites and thousands of other businesses and attractions that support nomadding including all this information would have required a substantially bigger book. Instead, we decided to create something truly unique. A book that would not only serve as a useful, standalone introduction but that would also allow you to access a huge amount of additional information.

This book includes an offer for Premium Membership to FRC which will allow you to access all areas of FRC's website and to use its app at a substantial discount.

Premium FRC Membership effectively allows you into a database of real-time, constantly updated information that is of immense value to nomads and all campers. Think of this book as a key that unlocks that database to you – and the main tools that you'll be using are the internet and the FRC's website and app.

Imagine being able to drive anywhere and know instantly where the nearest campsites are. Imagine being able to know exactly if they're free or paid and if so, how much you will have to pay. Imagine being able to phone them ahead to book a space. Imagine being able to find petrol stations, towing services, mechanics and suppliers and being able to get discounts on services and products. All this at the touch of a button, without having to spend frustrating hours looking through the internet, because we've already done all that work for you.

So, what you're holding in your hands is a tool that harnesses the full power of both the traditional printed word and the power of modern technology in an easy, accessible way. You don't have to imagine it anymore, because it's here, now, for you.

Happy camping! Happy nomadding!

And tell us what you think. We'd love to hear from you.

info@fullrangecamping.com.au
You'll find full details on FRC's Exclusive Offer for Premium Membership to readers of this book on page 318.

Three faces of Australia. The continent is so vast, so varied, that this, one of
the many waterfalls in the apple isle of Tasmania, is just as Australian as ...

this view of the iconic Kings Canyon in the Northern Territory …

… and this view of Esperance in WA, boasting the whitest sand of any beach in Australia. And they're all waiting for you to discover them.

Below: Beach on Fraser Island, Queensland, Australia.

PART ONE

FIRST STEPS

//

Grey Nomadding: Unleashing Your Inner Nomad

A grey nomad is defined as a retired person, usually over the age of fifty-five, who has chosen a life of travelling around Australia, exploring this amazing country's 7.692 million square kilometres (that's almost 3 million square miles). You could explore a thousand square kilometres of it every single day and it would still take you over twenty years to see all of it – and that's just the land. The coasts and waters are another thing altogether!

It's a life dominated by driving to far-flung places and either parking the recreational vehicle of your choice at a campsite or in the wild. It's a life of as much self-sufficiency and isolation or as much cooperation and community as you want. And it's a life of experiences and adventures that you couldn't possibly have any other way.

Grey nomads often travel in pairs, but singles and small groups of friends or family are not unknown, and all are bound by a common desire to experience Australia the way that they want to, in their own time and on their own terms.

Australia has several advantages as a place where you can adopt the grey nomad lifestyle:

- It is a developed, first-world economy with substantial infrastructure in place.
- It has a comprehensive health care system that includes emergency services that can reach most parts of the continent and its islands.
- It includes eight major climactic zones, ranging from tropical to alpine and thus supports a wide variety of plant and animal life as well as having some of the world's most spectacular scenery.
- It combines urban areas of dense population with vast, wild areas that are virtually uninhabited – and everything in between.
- It is one of the safest countries in the world to travel in and the wars, riots and other civil disturbances that plague so many other places on this planet are almost unknown here.
- It has one of the most comprehensive social security systems in the world, allowing even people of modest means to be able to afford the lifestyle.

It's unlikely that you'll choose this way of living unless there's always been a bit of a nomad inside you, waiting to get out – out of a city or a town, out of a rut or out of a way of living that isn't working for you anymore. If you're reading this, odds are you've felt that urge to break free and to unleash that inner nomad and begin your adventure.

You know you want to.

This guidebook is all about how you're going to make it happen so that the experience is one of the best of your life.

e longest journey starts with a footstep ... or at the very least a cup of tea.

Why Become Nomadic?

There are as many reasons to become a grey nomad as there are grey nomads, but some of the more common reason are:

- Liberation: from a mortgage, from the city or, sometimes, from relationships.
- Curiosity: about the country, about other people, or about themselves.
- Independence – a desire to be entirely self-determined, without anyone telling you what to do, whether it's a boss, a landlord or controlling families.
- Self-sufficiency: a need to experience what life is like when you rely mainly on your own resources and inventiveness, rather than the support of civilisation, to get through the day.

- Freedom: to have the time and means to experience difference – food, entertainment, scenery and the way that other people live – experiences that would be difficult to have if you were 'settled', or always bound to a particular time and place, and don't forget …
- Livin' the dream: for many, nomadding is the opportunity to fulfil a decades-long ambition to retire from the rat race and have a fun life of adventure. If not you, who? If not now, when?

This book is full of warnings and advice to be cautious, but the point is to be fully prepared. Yes, stuff happens, but it's still a fun and liberating life full of adventure. Our mission is simply to prepare you for some reversals, simply so that you can spend the vast majority of your time enjoying yourself. The fun part, after you've sorted out the basics, is up to you. Your own personal discoveries – that's where the real adventure is.

What's in a Name?

We can thank documentary filmmakers Catherine Marciniak and Steve Westh for coining the term 'grey nomad' in their documentary of the same name, first broadcast on ABC television on 23 September 1997. More than twenty years later, the term has not only gained a foothold in the Australian vernacular, and an entry in the *Macquarie Dictionary*, but in the consciousness of Australians as a whole. It's highly likely that you know at least one full-time or part-time grey nomad, maybe more.

You might still occasionally hear the word 'sundowner'. In past times in Australia, sundowners were travelling workers and odd-jobs men who'd arrive at farms too late to do any work, but who were happy to accept a meal and a place to sleep, so that at least they could start the next day rested and refuelled. The term doesn't quite have the same ring to it, nor does it sound as romantic as 'grey nomad'.

In North America, you'll hear the term 'snowbird'. This refers to retired people who travel south for a warmer climate during the winter months. It doesn't quite have the same implications as 'grey nomad' either.

It looks as if the name, as well as the phenomenon, is here to stay.

Strangely enough, some people who fit the description of grey nomad, absolutely hate the term, and especially hate the term being applied to them. Why this would be so is difficult to fathom, since most grey nomads wear the label with considerable pride, especially when you consider that being a *successful* grey nomad, with all its challenges, pitfalls and potential traps, is quite an achievement. But people are entitled to their eccentricities and it takes all types to make a world. Just be aware that not everyone who to all intents and purposes is a grey nomad, likes being called one, and be prepared for a negative reaction. It's rare, but these reactions do happen.

In any case, as you'll soon discover, there are a lot of different nomads out there, and they're not all grey.

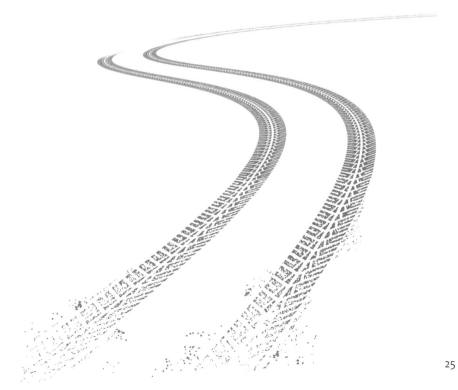

International Grey Nomads

What might have started off as a uniquely Australian way of living is now spreading to other countries, particularly the United States, but while an increasing number of Americans are enjoying what their own immense country has to offer, a lot of them are coming to Australia to explore the delights of the Great Southern Land and its own unique attractions.

International visitors on camping holidays to Australia are now at about 400,000 per year, clocking up an impressive five million camping nights. That's more than twelve nights per camper per year.

And it's not just Americans. In fact, the majority of visiting campers are from the UK and Germany although there is a small but growing number of Chinese visitors too, eager to experience Australia in a way that only camping can offer.

You'll never know who you're going to meet on your travels.

The Different Styles of Nomad

Nomads are just like everybody else, except that the nomadic lifestyle tends to bring out the more extreme version of who you already are with all the advantages and disadvantages that that implies. There are a few broad approaches to life, and they're all represented in the nomad population.

Mr and Ms Spontaneity

No planning, no forethought, no thinking ahead, just impulse. This is the nomad who wants the 'ultimate freedom' without bounds and limitations.

Advantages: serendipity and surprise, because anything can happen anytime and there's a certain feeling of romantic adventure to everything that happens because, when you live like this, everything is just so fresh, new and surprising.

Disadvantages: unpreparedness, which, in Australia, when combined with unfettered impulse, might result in clueless and fatal forays into genuine danger. Having said that though, unpreparedness more often than not just leads to unnecessary headaches and drama.

Best suited: for those who stay somewhat on the beaten track where more, shall we say, 'conscientious' people who think things through more thoroughly can rescue them if Mr and Ms Spontaneity get into too much trouble through lack of forethought.

Mr and Ms Prepared-for-Anything

The possessors of lots of 'things'. This nomad is extremely well-equipped for a broad range of eventualities and often has the latest state-of-the-art camping paraphernalia and creature comforts.

Advantages: if there's a problem, they usually have the right tool, piece of equipment or supply to fill the need or solve the problem.

Disadvantages: since there are so many things that *might* happen, or things you *might* need, it usually means lugging around a lot of stuff and you need to have a vehicle that can handle this and the budget for the increased petrol costs.

Best suited: for those who seek security in things and who don't feel that they have to compromise on comfort or security when they're away from civilisation. It also helps to have deep pockets for all the extra expenses incurred in lugging around so much stuff.

Mr and Ms Organised

While 'the spontaneous' should be prepared to live on beans (because they've run out of anything else) and 'the prepared' won't be able to do without their portable television sets and frozen, gluten-free bread, 'the organised' prefer to have the best of both worlds, but this means having to think ahead and doing some research. It's likely if your reading this that you're an 'organised', or you have an organised friend who has given you this book in the hopes that your adventure won't hurt you or kill you unnecessarily. The prepared will have this book, just in case, but have never read it and will only read it when they have to, and the spontaneous might have bought this book on impulse, but they have misplaced it and forgotten about it, because they got distracted by some shiny thing somewhere, which could be why you're reading it now, having picked it up where they left it behind.

Advantages: they've done the homework so are less likely to get into trouble and are less likely to have to carry around so much.

Disadvantages: might fall into the trap of being *over*-organised, with a timetable that has no flexibility or give. You might then get upset if you don't get to that music festival right on time. Or you might miss that spectacular sunset because you're too busy looking at the map.

Best suited: for those who have confidence in their ability to do the necessary research and planning, but who also know that they can improvise if something doesn't go exactly to plan. We hear this a lot about people who micro-plan their trip, then put so much pressure on themselves when they fail to see things, or don't allow much time to enjoy simple things or to stop and smell the roses.

The Big Pluses of the Nomad Way of Life

There's no doubt that nomadding is very attractive to a lot of people, otherwise there wouldn't even be a term for this way of living. Some of the pluses include:

- You're not tied down to any particular place because you have a lease or a mortgage that you're obliged to maintain.
- You're not tied down to any time because you're retired or have a super-flexible job, either because you can take your job anywhere (it can all be done on a laptop) or there's a need for you even in more remote or far-flung places (you're an agency nurse or a freelance electrician).
- You're not answerable to anyone, because you've either freed yourself from relationship obligations (boss/employee) or your relationships have evolved (parent/grown-up children).

- There are so many amazing experiences that you could have, but they won't come to you, you have to go to them and this lifestyle helps you do that.
- The opportunity for personal growth is there if you want it. You'll often find yourself doing things you never thought you would do or were even capable of doing. You'll discover potential that you might not have known you had. You'll become a different, and, if you do it right, a better version of yourself – more resourceful, more resilient, more capable and more confident.

One of the best things you can do to boost confidence in this whole nomadding, camping thing is to do a bit of rehearsal, in fact, a *lot* of rehearsal. Practice makes perfect, especially if you've never done anything like this before.

Are You One Too? Is This for You?

Nomadding is not for everyone. If it were, everyone who could be doing it, would be doing it. It's important to get real here. Unlike the romantic reputation it often has, the reality of nomad life is not one that is entirely free, or free of obligation, responsibilities or challenges.

You still have to follow traffic rules and if you drink, you have to stay under the legal limit because if you get caught, there goes your driver's licence. You still have to clean up after yourself when you visit a campsite because if you don't and a ranger catches you then here comes a fine. You'll still have to remember your friends and grandchildren's birthdays because if you don't here comes the guilt.

Exchanging One Set of Obligations, Responsibilities and Challenges for Another

Nomadding comes with certain responsibilities. These aren't just 'social' responsibilities, like remembering to send Christmas cards, these are responsibilities that your life might depend on – things you can't ignore. So, for example:

- You don't have the luxury of ignoring vehicle maintenance or forgetting to fill the gas tank or, even perhaps more critically, the water tank.
- You don't have the luxury of ignoring your health – like ignoring that persistent toothache or forgetting the use-by dates in the supplies in the first-aid kit, because things long ignored might become critical when you're far from help.
- You don't have the luxury of ignoring unresolved relationship problems because, if you're stuck in your van for a week in the rain they *will* come out – and it won't be pretty.

And nomadding presents all sorts of challenges that the more settled hardly ever need to think about, like having to put up with three different sets of neighbours in a week, or weather extremes, or the bites and stings of dangerous animals, breaking down in the middle of nowhere, or arguably worse, in the middle of a verybusy somewhere, or just plain getting lost.

The reality of nomadding is that, even though you're abandoning the obligations, responsibilities and challenges of 'normal life' – and 'good riddance' you might well say – you are exchanging those for another set of obligations, responsibilities and challenges.

Key Questions You Need to Ask Yourself

It's our hope that in reading this book you'll find out about a lot of things that you didn't know before. With new knowledge comes questions – lots of them. But the big questions that you have to ask yourself are these: Which sets of obligations, responsibilities and challenges do I prefer? Which are more fun, or, at the very least, more tolerable?

Deciding to become nomadic is a major decision. It requires a considerable lifestyle change. Changes will happen in your mind, heart and body, before during and after the transition from 'settler' to 'nomad'. Some people think that going nomad is one of the best decisions that they ever made. Others find themselves, after a few months, thinking to themselves, 'This is a complete disaster! What *were* we thinking?'

You can save yourself a lot of time, money, pain, suffering and hardship, and you can enjoy yourself a lot more too, if you think all this through first. If this book makes you think, helps you to make informed decisions, it will have done its job. And on the plus side, it's really rare that anyone regrets the decision to go nomadding. The vast majority of the time, whether people have prepared or not, the general nomad advice to those thinking about taking the plunge is to just do it, and not to sweat the small stuff.

Deal Killers

Let's start with some potential deal-killers and see if they apply to either you or your partner(s) or companion(s).

If you hate travelling, don't do this. This might seem obvious, but if your idea of 'travelling' has always been trotting around on carefully curated tours and which involve staying in five-star resorts, then nomadding isn't exactly the same thing. Even glamping (high-end camping with all-mod cons) isn't the same thing. Nomadding isn't usually associated with champagne breakfasts and jacuzzis, although there's no reason, in theory, why it can't be (as it is in glamping). Nomadding isn't even regular camping, it's a long-term commitment, or, at the very least, a series of medium-term commitments. Nomadding isn't tourism, it's *real* travel. It's feeling the bumps on the road, every single one of them, both literally and figuratively.

If you're a clean-freak, don't do this. If you're the sort of person who needs three hot showers a day just to feel vaguely human, things are going to get rough for you unless you're prepared for a large campsite bill in order to access enough water. For more about nomadding and hygiene, go to page 206.

If you *only* like the finer things in life, don't do this. If you're the sort of person who'll use any old type of tissues, you'll be fine, but if you always need to have aloe vera-impregnated pre-softened tissues scented with honeysuckle, you might run into some difficulty. Nevertheless, there are lots of things that you can do to maintain some level of creature comforts. Furthermore, if you have a strong sense of visual aesthetics you will be alternately thrilled at some breathtaking landscapes and wildlife and disgusted by the sight of flabby, over-tanned human bodies letting it all hang out in football shorts and thongs. Be psychologically prepared for both.

If you have no mechanical aptitude, think very carefully about this. There might be times when you'll have to do some sort of makeshift repairs and if mechanical devices are alien to you then you could find yourself in trouble you can't easily get out of. For more about nomadding and technology, go to page 193.

If you have a low tolerance for people, think very carefully about where you go and when. Nomadding often involves getting in the thick of things and it isn't always romantic skinny-dipping in isolated lakes fed by waterfalls or staring into the beauty of a sunset with your partner on an isolated beach. It can involve being in a crowded trailer park listening the whole night to the snoring of the fellow camper in the caravan next to you, or the early morning screams of the six kids in the family in the big rig on the other side of you. Sure, you can avoid this, but you have to plan to avoid it. Getting away from cities doesn't necessarily mean getting away from people and it can be especially tough if you find your boundaries violated by a party of drunken louts. For more about nomadding, dealing with people and human relationships in general, go to page 90.

If you have a pet, you're going to be restricted. Your beloved pooch might not be as adored everywhere else as it is at home. Cats are a different story, but they have their plusses and minuses too. For more about nomadding with your pets, go to page 106.

If you have a chronic health condition you have to plan carefully. If you're in the middle of nowhere, or even if you're in the middle of somewhere where everything's closed on the weekends, you're not going to be able to just run down to the corner chemist for your blood pressure medicine or your pain management. For more about nomadding and health, go to page 81.

One thing that we'd really like to emphasise: do *not* let your health condition stop you from travelling and making the most of your nomadic years. Most conditions are manageable and, luckily for you, it's likely that you'll find someone who is in a very similar position to you, who has a lot more experience and who would be more than happy to share what they've learned to make things easier.
You could also read Joy's story. Joy was told that she'd never walk again, but that didn't stop her *and* she had a dog too:
www.frc.camp/joystory
See also how seventy-five year old Kel, a man with paralysis *and* a tumour could still live it up:
www.frc.camp/meetkel

If you're underfinanced, or you haven't properly budgeted – which isn't the same thing – you're asking for a bunch of needless headaches. Nevertheless, if you plan properly, nomadding is cheaper than a settled life. For more about money go to page 45 and 70.

And if you're worried about it being the 'perfect time', stop. Stop that right now! Stop!

There will never be a 'perfect time'. But there will be a right time, and sooner than you might think.

Get used to not having 'all mod cons' all the time.

Getting Advice

It's amazing how many people make a major life change without doing their homework first and when things go pear-shaped, they wonder what went wrong, or when an opportunity comes up, they wonder why nobody told them.

The common response to people complaining that 'Nobody told me!' is 'You didn't ask.' So ask. But there has to be some method to your madness when it comes to doing your research on nomadism.

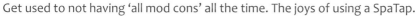
Get used to not having 'all mod cons' all the time. The joys of using a SpaTap.

Part of that method involves getting good advice and when getting advice, it's important that you consider the following:

- The half-baked, uninformed opinions of your ignorant friends, however well-meaning, are useless and only reveal their own prejudices. The well-considered, informed opinions of your knowledgeable friends are worth paying close attention to. Learn to tell the difference.
- Talk to people who have a lot of experience in the specific field that you're interested in. There's no point in talking to a refrigerator expert about solar panels – unless they happen to be experts in both, which is very possible – nevertheless, stick to advice from people within their specialty.
- Talk to people who have no vested interest in selling you one particular solution over another. Admittedly, this can be tricky as many genuine experts became genuine experts because they had vested interests in the first place.
- Notwithstanding the point about vested interests, some expert opinions are worth paying for – particularly financial advice and other advice given in a professional context. Many professional advisors are personally liable if they give bad advice, so it's in their interests to give you the best information that they can.
- In some cases, you might want advice from someone who doesn't normally sell their advice but is nevertheless very knowledgeable in their field. In such cases, it's courteous to offer to pay them for their time. A penny spent today could save you pounds in the future.
- Advice is only useful if you actually use it, so if you get really good advice and you ignore it and then come to grief, you've only got yourself to blame.

Some More of the Great Pluses

The nomad lifestyle lends itself beautifully to getting back in touch with things. After a lifetime of being so busy dealing with one mini-crisis after another and looking after other people's needs nomadding gives you the space to stop *doing* so much and to just be. It's particularly good for letting go of the past, letting the future take care of itself and just allowing yourself to enjoy the present moment. And if you've never meditated before, maybe now's the time to start, especially when you're in beautiful places, surrounded by peace and tranquillity, here and now is the time to give your soul some much-needed rest and relaxation.

After a lifetime of doing for others, an opportunity for some 'me time'. Finally!

The grey nomad and camping community as a whole is a sharing one. It's like this vast country town spread out around the whole

nation. Many in that community will generously and freely give you their valuable advice as long as you're sincere and obviously not a time-waster. The ethic of the camping community as a whole is that 'we're all in this together' and 'we've all been there'. So it's expected as a courtesy that one day, when you're more experienced, you'll 'pay it forward' and generously and freely give your time and advice to a newbie in the same way that when you were a newbie more experienced people were generous with their knowledge.

This is your choice, of course. Do what you like. It's your karma.

For more, check out FRC's Help Outs section:

www.frc.camp/helpingout

PART TWO

REDESIGNING, REINVENTING, RENEGOTIATING

///

Redesigning Your Life

It might seem strange to talk about 'designing' or 'redesigning' your life. For most people, life is what happens to them while they're making plans for something else. For most people, their lives aren't something they think of as something that can be 'designed'. But all 'design' means is rearranging your circumstances to make it as easy as possible for you to have the experiences that you want to have. In practical terms, this means having arrangements in place and access to the resources you need to help make things happen.

Going nomad is a big step, but it doesn't have to be one huge leap all at once.

Temporary or Permanent?

One thing needs to be clear: nomadding doesn't have to be all or nothing. So often people tend to make major life decisions on an either/or basis, and this limits their options and their thinking. But nomadding doesn't have to be like that. Depending on your individual circumstances you can ease into it, test it, give it a try before you commit. Even the commitment doesn't have to be all or nothing. There's nothing stopping you from being a part-time nomad or occasional nomad. Full-time nomads aren't 'better' than part-timers. Everyone is entitled to make choices that work for them.

Like, part-time nomads Aliza and Clarke (see below) or Peter and Dawn, who live in their caravan even when they are 'home' at their base-camp property:

www.frc.camp/peteranddawn

Aliza and Clarke – Part-time Nomads

Clarke, a retired manager, and Aliza, a part-time medical receptionist still working several days a week, weren't in a bad position. The house was fully paid for. They had an investment flat that was rented out to reliable tenants. Their son had moved out and their daughter was working part-time, studying part-time and still living at home. They had done camping trips in the past as a family and had enjoyed them but that had never been for more than a couple of weeks at a time. They knew that they wanted to give grey nomadding a try, but they weren't quite sure that they were ready to go 'all the way'.

They realised that they had enough money so that they could buy themselves a caravan and a sturdy vehicle to tow it around. They planned a year-long adventure that wouldn't take them too far off the beaten track but would still give them the chance to have a whole bunch of new experiences.

The realised that they didn't have to sell the house or spend a fortune on their rig (page 115). They were healthy and able-bodied and looked into ways that they could earn extra cash on the road (pages 58 to 69), but they knew that they could still make at least a year work without them having to earn any extra money at all. They knew that their kids would be OK without them. Most importantly, they had the security of knowing that if the whole nomadding thing didn't work out, then at any point on the journey, they'd still have a house to come back to and a bunch of memories, both good and bad, and nobody would ever be able to take that away from them.

Obviously, not everyone is in the same position as Aliza and Clarke, and some might even think that because they always had a way out that this wasn't a *real* test and so they wouldn't be truly committed to

Shutting the door on one life means opening a door to another, and that means planning.

nomadding, either physically or psychologically. But people vary in the way that they make life changes and some people are simply more cautious than others. Some people are happy taking 'baby steps'. In fact, one of the most frequently cited regrets that grey nomads have is that they transitioned too quickly and, if they could do it over, they would take things with a bit less rush. And, frankly, if you can be a nomad *and* have a settled option – if you have your cake and eat it too – why not?

Aliza and Clarke had no way of truly knowing what the experience was going to be like for them personally until they actually did it. No matter how many (excellent) guidebooks you read, (brilliant) websites you visit, documentaries and YouTube videos that you watch, or people that you talk to, in the end, your experience is your own.

But at least Aliza and Clarke were working on a tried-and-true principle of any project or venture: those who fail to plan, plan to fail.

So, let's talk a little about planning, particularly financial planning.

Financing the Life

A lot of people begin considering the nomad life when a whole bunch of circumstances hit them at the same time. This is the perfect storm of influences that take you into a life of nomadism.

Not all of the reasons we outline below apply to everyone, but here are the more common elements of the perfect nomad storm.

- Work life has finished: you've reached retirement and superannuation or the pension now kicks in. You've been retrenched or 'phased out' and you've gotten a big payout. You've lost your job for some other reason, and you're at that age where you're 'unemployable'. You've sold your business, or you've given it to your children, and you've come to a point where you feel that the rest of your life can be one long holiday.
- The house is paid off or, it seems, will never be paid off. Or you've been renting and you're wondering whether or not to renew the lease.

- The children are all grown up, even that thirty-something kid who never looked as if he was going to leave has finally landed on his feet and moved out.
- You've been sitting on all sorts of adventure dreams for decades and now, finally you have the time and the means to make them happen.

But the decision of whether or not to go nomad hinges, like most things, on the bottom line.

Is this actually affordable?

Will it work, first and foremost, *financially?*

Financial Planning and Financial Literacy

In principle, financial planning is simply the relationship between income and outgoings. And while this might seem simple there are traps for the unwary, so it pays (literally) to be financially literate.

You can define financial literacy as the ability to make informed choices about money, in particular how you can manage your personal finances in an efficient manner. In other words, when you have financial literacy you know how to use money without wasting it. If you're really good, you know how to use money to make money.

Half of all Australians (and we can assume half of everyone who lives in a country with a developed economy) struggle with financial literacy. This isn't just a made-up statistic, it comes from the HILDA study (Household, Income and Labour Dynamics in Australia), which the University of Melbourne has been conducting since 2001. In 2019 they asked their 17,500 participants the following questions. The answers are on page 309 but try not to cheat. See how many you get right:

1. Suppose you put A$100 into a no-fee savings account, with a guaranteed interest rate of 2 per cent per year. You don't make any further payments into this account and you don't withdraw any money. How much would be in the account at the end of the first year, once the interest payment is made?

2. Imagine now that the interest rate on your savings account was 1 per cent per year and inflation was 2 per cent per year. After one year, would you be able to buy more than today, exactly the same as today, or less than today with the money in this account?

3. Do you think that the following statement is true or false? 'Buying shares in a single company usually provides a safer return than buying shares in a number of different companies.'

4. Again, please tell me whether you think the following statement is true or false? 'An investment with a high return is likely to be high risk.'

5. Suppose that by the year 2020 your income has doubled, but the prices of all of the things you buy have also doubled. In 2020, will you be able to buy more than today, exactly the same as today, or less than today with your income?

[Source: www.intheblack.com/articles/2019/02/01/australians-struggle-financial-literacy-retrieved 20190704]

The good news is that the survey discovered that the grey nomad demographic was likely to get all five answers correct, but if you didn't, don't despair. It just means you have some work to do. Even if you did get all five answers correct, don't get too smug, you probably still have some work to do.

Why is this talk about finance important? Because grey nomads can't afford to be financially illiterate. *When you run out of money, you run out of options.*

And while the various points about money that we make throughout this guide won't be a comprehensive overview of financial literacy, the information that follows throughout the book is here particularly with the grey nomad in mind, so that you don't make some elementary and stupid mistakes, and so that you can spend less time thinking about money and managing it (boring!) and more time thinking about your adventures and then experiencing them (exiting!).

Basic Questions You Need to Ask

Assume the following, even if all the following assumptions don't apply to you:

- You will be going nomad full time.
- You have to buy *all* of your equipment, including your rig.
- Your income will be whatever it is from superannuation, your pension or other assets and *not* supplemented by additional work.
- Your expenses will be based entirely on the nomad lifestyle.
- Any assets that you do have, such as investment properties etc. are paying for themselves and need no further contribution from you.

Now ask yourself these questions:

- What is the yearly household income?
- How much money do you have on hand now?
- How much money will there be left over after all the equipment is paid for?
- What will the running costs of everything be? This includes petrol and all other vehicular expenses which might even include water and electricity.
- What will the maintenance costs of everything be? And by 'maintenance of *everything*' we mean everything, including maintaining *you*.
- What are your shelter expenses? Sure, you'll have your RV or equivalent, but what if you want to stay at campsites, or even, now and then, in a hotel?
- What are your food and clothing expenses?
- Basic cleaning, grooming and medical expenses?
- Pet expenses?
- What about entertainment expenses? Not everything is free and even a quick beer at an outback pub is an entertainment expense.

- How much money is there in the emergency kitty?
- What about insurance and roadside assistance memberships?

If you've ever applied for a home loan, you'll note that the questions on the application for the loan are basically the same as those above. This is because the decision to go nomad shouldn't be taken lightly or casually and the basic assumption that you can't live beyond your means is the same.

If you've never thought about your finances this deeply before, we suggest that you start doing so now.

Remember that there are basically three types of costs:

1. **Asset costs.** These are the costs of your equipment, everything from you rig and fit-out to a teaspoon sitting in a drawer.
2. **Fixed costs.** These are the costs that have to be paid no matter what, like motor vehicle registration and insurance.
3. **Variable costs.** These are costs that have some give in them, depending on what you do. For example, you might end up with lower electricity costs if your rig has solar panels installed. You might save on gas costs if you do a lot of campfire cooking. However do note that even 'variable' costs usually have a defined lower limit.

Obviously, you won't be able to answer all those questions immediately, because the answers will depend on information you might not have or decisions that you haven't made … yet. But whatever you do, you can't avoid these questions and still hope that you can successfully redesign your life to be a successful nomad.

If you'd like a further insight as to how one couple managed their expenses, have a look at Terry and Jerry's Oz adventure:

www.frc.camp/ozadventure

Grey Nomadding and Centrelink

Australia has a social security system that's the envy of a lot of the world. Poverty still exists in Australia, but 'poor' in Australia doesn't exactly mean the same thing as 'poor' in, say, Mozambique.

The system isn't perfect, but state pensions allow two million older Australians – 7 per cent of the population – to live in *relative* comfort; at least by world standards.

But part of the price older Australians pay for their pensions is having to deal with what used to be called the Department of Social Security but since 1997 is called the Department of Human Services – Centrelink.

The grey-nomad life can be a relatively inexpensive one, but it still needs to be saved for and properly budgeted for.

Many find dealing with Centrelink intimidating and bureaucratic but dealing with Centrelink is something that you have to do if you want to be a grey nomad on an age pension. Stories about dealing with Centrelink range from recurring nightmares to dream runs of people doing everything in their power to help you.

Centrelink, like any organisation, is staffed by people. Staff have to deal with all sorts and some Centrelink clients are a lot worse than others. A little kindness and etiquette go a long way, believe us. In some cases, the courtesy that you show might be the brightest thing in some overworked person's day and they'll appreciate being treated like a human being rather than like some faceless bureaucrat.

If you want to make your dealings with Centrelink as smooth as possible, it helps to have some foreknowledge about what your entitlements and obligations are as an aged pension recipient. At the time of writing, to receive an age pension in Australia, you have to be aged sixty-five years or older. By 2023, you'll need to be sixty-seven.

Like any government set up, the rules change depending on who's in government at the time, how badly they want to keep the senior vote, and which way the wind is blowing, but the following information was current as at 1 July 2019 and provides a rough guide for planning.

Age pensions are means tested. If you have too many assets, you get a reduced pension, or no pension at all. The means test looks at your income (from various sources, including superannuation and investments) and your assets – both liquid (how much money you have squirrelled away in bank accounts) and the 'estimated assessed' value of non-liquid assets (including your car(s), investment properties and even estimates on the value of your personal possessions.

Important point: The home you live in, your primary residence, is not means tested – it is considered an *exempt* asset. The Australian government doesn't expect you to sell your house in order to get a pension. But other assets count as part of the means test.

- If you're a single homeowner your other assets can't exceed a value of $258,000 before those assets affect your full pension.
- If you're a homeowner couple, your other assets combined can't exceed a value of $387,500 before those assets affect your full pension.
- If you're a single non-homeowner your total assets can't exceed a value of $465,500 before those assets affect your full pension.
- If you're a non-homeowner couple, your total assets combined can't exceed a value of $594,500 before those assets affect your full pension.

Note the point about your assets affecting a *full* pension. Your assets can be more if you're happy to settle for a part-pension, but there's an upper limit to those too before you can't get an age pension at all. After all, the age pension isn't supposed to be for the rich.

And to repeat, the house you live in is an *exempt* asset. You can, theoretically, live in a $10 million house and it won't affect your pension. It happens; sometimes children of relatively modest means inherit properties that are worth a lot of money. They become the cash poor/asset rich.

Whatever your circumstance, *you do not have to sell your house to become a grey nomad* and as long as your house is still your principle place of residence it's not an asset.

As a pensioner, of course, you're entitled to take extended holidays for as long as you like – as long as these are 'temporary absences'. However, if you're away for more than twelve months it's hard to argue 'temporary absence' and at this point Centrelink might question your living arrangements and decide that your rig is your permanent residence (and presumably, at that point, it becomes an exempt asset) and your house – your former permanent residence – becomes a means-tested asset.

Take note too that if your house is vacant while you're nomadding, or your non-rent-paying, freeloading children are still living at home, this isn't *necessarily* a problem, but if you're renting it out and getting an income then that income is part of the means test and it will affect your pension.

Centrelink has a free Financial Information Service that you might want to access. Meetings arranged with the service are confidential and the service is there to help you if you want to find a way of making sense of what can become a complex assessment process and to help you redesign your arrangements so that you don't miss out on entitlements. Their experts can also help you budget your life in terms of how much income you can earn (page 68) and how to meet any other financial obligations.

While the rules might look tricky, information is power, and when you apply imagination to information, you can come up with a creative solution.

Keeping a Bolthole

As we keep saying, there's not just one way to be a nomad. You don't have to sell up everything and commit completely to a life on the road, even if you are relying on an age pension entirely to fund your day-to-day living expenses. You might, for example, choose to sell the former family home and downsize to a modest apartment, granny flat or small house. This small house then becomes base camp.

Your base camp then might become your winter or summer bolthole, depending on what type of weather or climate that you like or like to avoid. Remember that your 'real home' will be that nice little rig you get for yourself. The other advantage of having a bolthole will be that you have some sort of place to settle down if or when you tire of nomadding. Even if you love nomadding, there will come a time, if you live long enough, when, as willing as the spirit might be, the body will stop cooperating and you will have to transition to a more settled existence.

Choose a charming country town somewhere and pick up a bargain. Australia has hundreds of charming 'undiscovered' country towns – friendly communities that are dying to have you. This isn't just an expression. Many rural communities are in fact dying as they lose population to the bigger towns and cities and they're willing to go to extra effort to encourage people to move in. You might find yourself in the middle of a rural renaissance, buying into a community that will welcome you with open arms. Choose carefully and you might end up somewhere that you'll love spending your later years too.

If you're already attracted to nomadding, you know that life isn't all about the big cities and that one of the best-kept secrets is that you can live an excellent life in a rural community. You don't have to skimp on anything either, as you'd be amazed at how well-resourced some places are and how many opportunities exist outside of the 'big twelve' most populous urban areas of more than 200,000 people. For more about regional businesses, visit FRC's Business Directory.

Your base camp doesn't have to be ultra-swish and you don't have to overcapitalise on it. After spending months in a motorhome even a small apartment or a cottage can seem huge. If you decide you adore your bolthole and you love your neighbours, you can still wait until later to renovate it for permanent living.

Of course, security might be an issue, so you might want to cultivate excellent relationships with your neighbours to keep an eye on your bolthole or invite friends or family to stay there on a regular basis so that you don't discover that vandals have wrecked the place or, worse, find out that squatters have moved in while you've been away.

Having a base camp also means paying rates, but these can be modest. Whatever the circumstances, you have to think these things through and consider all your options.

But if you work it right, then no matter which place you live in, you'll still be working within the arcane rules of Centrelink and still get a full age pension. Again, specific advice from an accountant, financial planner or Centrelink's Financial Information Service would be the best places to help you make a decision that can let you have as much of your cake as you can get and still eat it too.

A nice way to transition to nomadding is to sell up in the big city and downsize to a bolthole you can use as a 'base camp' to return to when you need a break from travelling.

The best of both worlds might still be yours. Maybe you can get yourself a nice little fixer-upper or a ready-to-move in.

A Note About Insurance

If you have a full-time home with contents insurance, some of this might cover your contents while on the road, but you'll have to check your policy.

Many caravan insurance companies do not cater for full-time travellers due to obscure technical reasons to do with having or not having a permanent fixed address. Some nomads have thus been forced to get around this by putting the address of a relative or friend on the application form, even if they only stay there one night a year. This is definitely a situation that needs attention, so FRC is in the process of setting up a new insurance policy that will cater for full-timers.

For further information go to: **www.frc.camp/insurance**

You do *not* want to be this person in this situation without insurance. Trust us. You don't.

Setting Up an Income Stream

There's more than one way to skin a cat, and there's definitely more than one way to set up an income stream but it's definitely something that you'll have to do in order to make the whole grey nomad thing work. Otherwise, you'll be watching your bank account gradually dwindle to nothing, and while some people can live pension to pension, living on the edge isn't for everyone.

Like everything else, an income stream doesn't have to be either/or. The suggestions below are just a guide but there's no one-size-fits-all solution and you're completely free to adopt a mixed strategy where you get income from a variety of different sources. You have options, you need to consider all of them and work out what's right for you.

Industry Super Funds and Self-Managed Super Funds (SMSFs)

If you've been thinking about your retirement for years, you've spent decades in regular employment and you've managed to squirrel away a nice little nest egg, then you'll either have a lot of that nest egg tied up in assets or an industry superannuation fund. As soon as you hit your magic retirement age, your superfund will be able to dole out some money to you. If it's not enough, your pension can supplement it.

If you're particularly savvy, you might also consider a self-managed super fund (SMSF). Without getting overly technical, a SMSF is a trust structure. It's an arrangement that enables you to have income-generating assets with serious tax advantages. The catch is that you can't access the funds until after you retire, but then, that's what you're planning for anyway. That's why SMSFs have two phases: an *accumulation phase* with a tax cap of 15 per cent and a *pension phase* that has no tax at all.

Because an SMSF is a trust, it requires a trustee – someone who makes the decisions on where the money goes, how it's invested and how the money is paid out. Two types of trustees are possible:

- Individual trustees: private individuals who control the trust. There have to be at least two of you.
- A company trustee: in which there's a company structure where each member of the trust is a director of the company.

Setting up and managing an SMSF is a bit of a job which comes with some legal obligations, but it does give you a lot of control over what you have and what you do with it. SMSFs give you a lot of flexibility, allowing you to respond rapidly to changes in the investment environment so that you can maximise your investment returns. You can also consolidate assets with other people and get considerable leverage combining forces.

SMSFs are not for everyone. In order to be worth doing, SMSFs need a starting balance of around $300,000 and the expectation that this fund will continue to grow. You are responsible for how your SMSF is structured so you've either got to know what you're doing or you'll need the help of reputable fund managers to give you the right advice so that you stay within the rules – being non-compliant leaves you open to heavy penalties. SMSFs have to be run by Australian residents so you can't have relatives living overseas as trustees. You're also responsible for dispute resolution and working out an exit strategy if, for any reason, you have to close the fund.

But if you can handle all that SMSFs are an excellent way of keeping control of your money and paying no tax during the pension phase of the fund – not even capital gains tax. Talk to your accountant or a specialist in the field to work out the best strategy for you.

Working for Dosh

The most obvious way of securing an income stream, and one that most of us are all too familiar with, is to, somehow, keep working for a living – exchanging your skills and labour for dosh. While working for a living might seem to fly in the face of the romantic ideal of a life of the endless 'holiday' of nomadding, working does have several advantages.

After a lifetime of work and the structure, meaning and purpose that work provides, there are a considerable number of people – in fact probably the majority of people – who don't adjust well to a 'life of leisure'. The reality is that the life of *pure* leisure is only really healthy and suitable for a small minority of people who have an inbuilt character for it. There's a reason that the spoilt rich kid who gets ruined with drugs, or superficial parasitic aristocrats are cultural stereotypes. Most people who have the option of not working don't have the temperament to stay healthy without some sort of work. A lot of people think that the rich spend all their time lounging around pools drinking daiquiris but in fact most of them are dedicated workaholics, and it's not necessarily because they like money (although, admittedly, a lot of them do) but because their work provides them with a sense of self-worth. The idle rich are often alcoholics or narcaholics destined for early graves because people seem to need stimulation from *something*.

The reality that 'retirement isn't all it's cracked up to be' seems to be particularly hard on men. Men tend to find meaning and validation through their work in a way that's different to women. Women on average live longer than men and while there might be many reasons for this, work and retirement might play some part in this. Having said that, there is an increasing body of evidence that retirement', especially early retirement, is actually hard on both sexes.

In addition:

- Working for money allows you to keep your existing skills and to add new ones.
- If the work is physical, you get all the benefits of exercise, without the expense of gym memberships.
- Working for money provides, obviously, supplementary income.
- It helps you maintain your social skills and expands your social network.

There are any number of interesting jobs you can do that will help you earn a little spending money and, with any luck, you can learn new skills.

- It helps you maintain a sense of usefulness, and that might be important for your self-esteem.
- Lastly, but by no means least, work can help stave off boredom. No matter how many adventures you might have in stunning nature or in charming country towns with eccentric and friendly locals, some people just like to work because work gives them a satisfaction that they can't get from anything else.

Busting the Myth of Unemployability

One of the biggest myths about people of grey nomadding vintage is that over fifty-fives are 'unemployable'. There is some evidence that prejudice against older workers exists in the cities but in regional Australia there is a *massive* skills shortage and if you have a skill in demand there's no reason to believe that you can't get well-paying work. Even unskilled work (if such a thing really exists, since all work requires some skill) is in high demand, especially at different times of the year. Farmers often need an extra pair of hands for odd jobs and many of them would much rather hire a healthy grey nomad over, say, a backpacker, because of the advantages of maturity and stability.

The demand for workers who have achieved some level of maturity is real enough to justify the creation of specialist websites for seniors, whether nomadic or not. Older Workers is a website that is, in their own words: 'Australia's only national job board connecting older job seekers to age-friendly employers. All job listings are from age-friendly employers looking for older workers. Experience, reliability, strong work ethic and mentoring skills are just some of the huge benefits older workers bring to an organisation. We have over 55,000 registered, mature age jobseekers ready to give businesses an edge by having an experienced and diverse workforce.'

You can register with them or browse their site at your leisure:

www.olderworkers.com.au

Another dedicated website, Grey Nomads Jobs, 'Find employment, jobs, house sitting and community opportunities with thousands of "nomad-friendly" employers all over Australia.' The site is also an opportunity for employers 'to tap in to the 80,000 strong mobile workforce that is travelling right now and looking for opportunities. A highly skilled and experienced workforce. People who not only want to work but also want to stop and stay a little longer.'

www.greynomadsjobs.com

The Grey Nomads website also has a page dedicated to work:

www.thegreynomads.com.au/lifestyle/working-as-you-go
www.seniors.com.au/superannuation/discover/
work-opportunities-for-seniors

Minding Your Own Business with Skills in Demand

Some aspiring nomads have always run their own businesses, so the idea of making an income from your own business won't be new. Others have been employees all their lives and have never really thought much beyond their roles in the businesses and organisations that they worked for.

But one of the recurring themes of nomadding is *independence* and there's no reason why you can't extend the principle of independence to your income stream too. Now might just be the time to get a little entrepreneurial. Feel free to link into the FRC network to find out about the opportunities that might be out there.

Setting up a business in Australia is relatively easy if the work is unregulated or does not require licensing or registration. Even if the work does require you to have a special qualification it might be worth getting, especially if you've always dreamed of doing a particular type of work. But let's assume simplicity.

You'll need an Australian Business Number or ABN for short. The advantage of getting an ABN is that the Australian Taxation Office then assumes that you're serious about making some money. It means that you can claim all business-related expenses, including goods and services tax (GST) if you register for GST. Speak to your accountant about how much of your transportation and other expenses you can claim. Getting an ABN is easy and you do it through the Australian Business Register: **www.abr.gov.au**

Having a business means keeping records and it also means taking out insurance, so it's a good idea to think about all this before you get up and go. You might consider taking some sort of small business course to educate yourself (page 199).

While it might be tempting to go 'cash in hand and off the books' this strategy comes with some risks. For starters, it's illegal, which should be enough of a reason. But even if it weren't, the biggest risk is liability. If, in the course of doing your work, you injure yourself or your clients or damage your own or their property and you're not properly covered by insurance then you're potentially in for substantial damages and *no insurance company will cover you if you're acting outside of the law.* That's just the reality.

Having said that, there are a number of both conventional and somewhat unconventional ways that you can make money running your own business as a grey nomad.

Trades and Professions

There is always a massive skills shortage in regional centres and in the country and if you think ahead and let it be known to the right people that you'll be in a particular place at a particular time then people will be beating a path to your door. While a list of the most sought-after skills and where they're needed would be the size of a book in itself you can get a lot of information about the current skills shortages that the Australian government has identified from the Department of Employment, Skills and Family Services' Skill Shortages Program:

www.docs.employment.gov.au/category/program-430
www.employment.gov.au/national-state-and-territory-skill-shortage-information

Stand-out skills shortages include:

- Childcare centre managers and childcare workers and teachers
- Nurses, midwives, optometrists, retail pharmacists and a host of other allied medical professionals and there's a growing demand for aged-care workers and special-needs workers, especially in regional areas
- Construction engineers, draftspersons and surveyors
- Automotive and engineering trades workers
- Construction trades workers
- Food trade workers, especially butchers, smallgoods makers, chefs and pastry chefs

- Cabinet makers, hairdressers and arborists

These skills shortages are chronic and have persisted for at least the last decade. They are so in demand that Australia actually has to import qualified people to fill the shortage, even people who are over forty-five and who wouldn't normally pass the current points test:

www.workpermit.com/immigration/australia/
australia-skills-shortage-list

It might seem a bit radical to re-educate or retrain yourself for work that's in demand, but if you're preparing for nomadding and there's work that you've always thought you'd like to try then there are a number of educational options, including online courses that you can invest a few months or even a few years in while you transition to nomadding. The option exists in many of these skills in demand for you to either be a short or long-term employee or for you to offer your services as a freelancer, billing for those services through your own business.

Thinking Outside the Conventional Work Box

If you step back a moment and look at the economy as a whole, you realise that it's made up of a population of people exchanging goods and services for other goods and services. Generally, money is involved, but only because it's a convenient way of translating one lot of goods and services for another. Sometimes the economy demands money and money is key. It doesn't matter how great a hairdresser you are, you can't pay your mortgage by offering to cut, colour and style the hair of your bank's employees. You need to translate your haircutting into money so that money can pay off your home loan. But nomadding offers a range of possibilities to exchange goods and services that are unavailable to the settlers. There is an abundance of available work out there, whether for the money or for the experience. Once people in the outback find out you're skilled, the job offers will come.

As a nomad, if there is work somewhere, you are mobile enough to go to it, even if it's in a remote location. Some businesses in particular find it hard to get much needed maintenance services done – think refrigeration services or think of a mobile knife-sharpening business for restaurants and food service businesses, or think of just general odd, handyperson or cleaning jobs you could offer. Think imaginatively. Think creatively. Think opportunistically.

Since you might not be tied down to a mortgage or a lease, you have the flexibility to take on seasonal, temporary, short-term or long-term jobs that are casual, part-time or full-time. Fruit picking is a classic seasonal, casual job but there's nothing stopping you from spending six months or a year in a lovely country town somewhere if there's a work contract that suits you. Since you've done your sums right (we hope) and you don't necessarily have to work, you're in a position of power to just walk away if the situation isn't win/win or if it no longer suits you. And remember that money doesn't always have to be involved.

If you get a bit sick of living in your RV and would like a solid roof over your head for a little while you could exchange food or board or both in exchange for housesitting or farmsitting. See the FRC website for more on this. Bartering for accommodation even has the government's stamp of approval; in Western Australia in particular you can be a camp host, collecting fees and having general overseeing duties in exchange for free camping. Volunteer work can also get you free camping and might lead to paid work too. Some volunteer programs even teach you new, tradeable skills. See also:

www.frc.camp/help@monkeymia

Nomad to Nomad

Nomads, just like everybody else, need things done and, arguably, who better to provide for those needs than fellow nomads? You'll see various forms of entrepreneurship all over the place, particularly in caravan parks. Here there'll be fellow nomads offering everything:

services from haircuts and manicures to massages and welding. There are even people who set up shops selling arts and crafts and, if you're a talented cook and you have the facilities, you might be able to knock up some delicious treats that would otherwise be hard to come by way out in the bush.

This is a win for you, because if you have a little business going you'll get to meet and network with a whole bunch of people, and business overheads in a caravan park aren't exactly onerous. This is a win for your clients, since they don't have to leave the park to get what they want or need.

But one downside is restrictions with the park management or owners, who, quite rightly, might have concerns about liability and legality. Here is where being legit offers you an advantage; if you can show that you're fully registered as a business and fully covered by insurance for what you do, then that's a powerful bargaining chip to get a 'yes'.

You don't even have to stick to one business. You can get a set of magnetic signs made up offering different services and if you get fed up providing one, you can take it off your RV and put up another, or none at all if you want to give yourself a break.

Clever ideas that require skills but few overheads are:
- Sewing and clothes repairs
- Vehicle maintenance, cleaning and upgrading, especially vehicle dustproof sealing
- Any specialist but tricky job that's really needed by people running RVs that even mechanics don't do too well, like repacking caravan wheel bearings
- Anything to do with technology, like fixing a remote internet connection or helping people to update their operating systems or even teaching people how to use apps.

To help you out even more, FRC offers a special service with its free business listings. It's a map marker, so if you're a travelling business all you do is update your location as you go and people can always find you. If you want some time off, just temporarily disable your listing, and when you're open for business again, just reenable it. Easy!

Just thinking outside of the box for the moment: Various forms of animal maintenance jobs are always in demand in the country. It might be worthwhile exploring various educational options or even a 'mature-age apprenticeship'. It might take a while to gain a qualification, but if you prepare now for later, who knows what opportunities might come your way?

Age Pensions, the Work Bonus and Income Limits

It's gradually dawning in the consciousness of various Australian governments that making it hard for pensioners to earn money while also being on the pension might not be the brightest of policies. Pensioners represent a vast pool of talent and experience and pensioners who earn money also have more money to spend, thus helping the economy.

In particular, it might also eventually occur to our beloved policy makers that grey nomads are in an excellent position to provide and use services in regional and remote communities, providing much-needed cash injections to more remote populations and the businesses that serve them. Grey nomads often talk about the warm fuzzy glow they get from helping out some of Australia's more far-flung communities, whether as workers or customers.

The pressure is on for pensioners to get a better deal, and the pressure is increasing, especially as their numbers grow. By 2040 there will be almost seven million over sixty-fives. A conservative estimate is that this will be at least *20 per cent of the population.* Show us an economy that can afford at least one in five people to be unproductive. Before you know it eighty will be the new sixty-five.

For the moment, Centrelink provides a work bonus as an incentive for pensioners to continue to participate in the workforce. The Work Bonus works like this: as at 2020 you can earn up to $250 per fortnight without that work affecting your pension. If you don't work, or if you earn less than that amount, any unused sum gets credited to you as part of the Work Bonus. Your Work Bonus gets capped at $6500. So, potentially, you could earn $125 per week, every single week of your life, and it wouldn't affect your pension. At the other end of the spectrum, you could do no work at all for a year, then, in one sudden week of tremendously productive and profitable activity, earn $6500, and it still wouldn't affect your pension.

Beyond the Work Bonus, the more you earn, the less money you'll get from an age pension. The upper limits of the government's generosity, and the point at which your pension disappears, is, for singles $49,000 per year, for couples $75,000 per year.

Saving Money and Financial Tips for the Thrifty

No matter how good you are with money or how financially literate, no income stream is unlimited. As Warren Buffet – a man who still eats cut lunches his wife makes – says, 'Even billionaires need to budget', so it's a good idea to save money when you can.

Grey nomads have a reputation in some quarters for being, well … how do we put this? … tight. This isn't necessarily because grey nomads don't want to spend money, but simply because they can't, because they're under-funded and maybe because their expenses are greater than what they originally imagined. Hopefully, the advice and knowledge that we're providing you in this guide will go a long way to prevent you from becoming a travelling pauper.

Notwithstanding, 'A penny saved is a penny earned' isn't just cheap philosophy, it's sensible practice. So, at the risk of teaching our grandmothers and grandfathers how to suck eggs, here are some tips to help you make those dollars stretch further. Some of these tips are obvious, some of them are not so obvious, and some specifically apply to the grey nomad. In no particular order of importance:

- Agree that your children are old enough not to require elaborate Christmas presents and be imaginative about the gifts you can give your grandkids. Remember, you have a whole continent to explore and who knows what you'll find for them.
- Buy second hand. It's amazing how often you can find high-quality stuff, especially clothing, in thrift stores. It's all about timing.
- Ditch the credit cards and use debit cards instead.
- Do most of your own cooking. Food is another major expense, so the more you save the more you can treat yourself when you do eat out.
- Get yourself a money box that you can't open until its full, like one of those tins you can buy at a two-dollar shop. If you just

put in your loose change you'd be surprised how much you end up with when it's full.

- Have some sort of budget and stick to it as closely as possible. Budgets are easy in principle but can be challenging to practice. One of the easiest ways to stick to a budget is to have a notebook in which you meticulously record everything you spend. The act of having to record what you spend somehow makes it real and memorable. When you record everything you become acutely aware of where all the money is going, and, to revisit a major theme of this book, because you're informed you can make informed choices.

- If you plan to stay in a particular area, join the local library to access all their books, music and movies. They also have free internet access!

- Keep everything well maintained, *particularly your RV and rig*. This can be something as simple as just keeping your engine's air filter clean – which is especially challenging in some of Australia's dust-ridden road conditions. A clean air filter can make up to a 10 per cent difference in fuel consumption, which is significant when fuel is a major expense.

- Make full use of every possible benefit offered by your Seniors Card (page 74).

- Make sure that you and your partner are on the same page when it comes to managing money. Money is a *major* reason couples fight (see page 101).

- Reduce or eliminate vices. Alcohol and driving don't mix and smoking is literally money up in smoke. If there was ever a time to get these vices under control, switching to nomadding would be it.

- Shop around for the best deals on major expenses like medical and vehicle insurance.

- Simplify your bank accounts. Many banks offer no-fee accounts to seniors.
- Stop spending money as a way of coping with stress. Theoretically, nomadding should mean a lot less stress anyway.
- Take advantage of sales, especially for food.
- Turn off heating and air conditioning when you're not using it or learn how to use timer functions so that your RV can be pre-heated or pre-cooled when you come back from an outing, without it needing to be on all day.
- Watch your mobile data allowance. It's amazing how often non-tech-savvy people get caught out paying for extra data because they don't understand how companies charge for mobile phones and internet access.
- And use the FRC app and Digital Member Discount Card to access offers and discounts as you travel. It's specifically designed for the traveller with RV-related businesses. Examples include 5 per cent discounts at participating IGA supermarkets, 10 per cent off at Battery World, 20 per cent off at Tint a Car, 10 per cent off at Kui Caravan Parks as well as over 600 other businesses currently offering discounts. And there's more on the way all the time.

There are dozens of ways to save money and resources. Talk to your fellow nomads; hard-won experience has probably taught them a trick or two that they'd love to share with you.

The Seniors Card

Seniors Cards are state-funded initiatives that provide a slew of benefits to the holder, including:

- Australia-wide travel concessions and in some cases the card is internationally recognised
- Discounts at tens of thousands of businesses and government-run organisations as well as on some fees, like vehicle registration (although this is not available in all states and territories)
- Special offers and competitions.

Because they're state-based, you need to apply for one based on a fixed, permanent residence, even if that residence is an address of one of your children, or a non-nomadic friend. All that's required is that you be over a particular age (at least sixty, and the eligibility age varies between states), are a 'permanent resident' of the state or territory in which you apply and be doing no more than a certain number of hours of work per week (e.g. twenty in New South Wales but thirty-five in Queensland).

Seniors cards are not *automatically* issued, and it takes up to four weeks for it to arrive. So, apply before you leave home by supplying

your postal address, your date of birth and your Medicare number as your ID is required in some states too.

No matter which state you have your Seniors Card in, there are reciprocal arrangements, so benefits are available all over Australia, and some even in New Zealand. You can select to be on an email list for regular updates about all sorts of deals and join in the fun of a Seniors Festival as you journey.

ACT: **www.actseniorscard.org.au**; 02 6282 3777

NSW: **www.seniorscard.nsw.gov.au**; 13 77 88

Northern Territory: **www.nt.gov.au/community/seniors/ apply-for-seniors-card**; 1800 441 489

Queensland: **www.qld.gov.au/seniors/legal-finance- concessions/seniors-card/applying-seniors-card**; 13 74 68

South Australia: **www.sa.gov.au/topics/family-and- community/seniors/seniors-card/apply-for-a-seniors- card**; 1800 819 961

Tasmania: **www.dpac.tas.gov.au/divisions/csr/programs_ and_services/seniors_card**; 1300 135 513

Victoria: **www.seniorsonline.vic.gov.au/seniors-card**; 1300 797 210

Dying to Get Away

No discussion of nomadding and finances would be complete without at least a passing mention about making suitable provisions if, by chance, in the course of your nomadding, you shuffle off the mortal coil. Whether or not you want to have the discussion, and no matter how awkward it might be, it's a conversation that's responsible to have. Your death would be traumatic enough for your family and other loved ones even under 'normal' circumstances, but if you are thousands of kilometres away the scenario could be fraught with complications.

Preparation is key here. So:

- Have your affairs in order. Have your last will and testament up to date and legally enforceable.
- Have fully paid-up funeral insurance or a funeral plan. Make sure that the plan covers the transport of your body back home and that all 'disposal costs' are covered.
- Have some sort of list made up of people who need to be informed. Your children won't necessarily know the names and contact details of all your friends and family, especially if your family is spread out internationally.
- One positive thing about dying is that you get to have the last word and, if your family is full of juicy secrets, a chance to make all those revelations that were waiting until all the concerned parties are gone. Writing a document filled with your final thoughts, wishes and family gossip might be something that you'll enjoy!

One useful way of being organised about all this is to purchase a kit. We strongly recommend *The Will Kit and My Final Thoughts and Wishes* (**www.au.newhollandpublishers.com/the-will-kit-plus-my-final-thoughts-and-wishes.html**).

It might be worth mentioning repatriation here. One of the biggest concerns that family and friends have is getting someone home either when they're sick or when they've passed away. Many of the standard caravan insurance policies out there do not cover this. And many of the people in the nomadding community people don't even know that covering the expenses of repatriation is an available insurance option. Once again, FRC has your back, and they include it as part of their insurance options. The FRC Repatriation Option allows for repatriation not only of a insured person, but anyone else in their travelling party too. So if, say, one partner has a heart attack, the option will cover the cost of getting both partners home, as well as costs incurred for getting the RV or rig back too, in case both parties need to return in a hurry. Similarly, if Granny and Gramps take the grandkids camping, and one of the kids breaks a leg and they all need to go home, they'll all be covered too. As you can see, this option is useful to both the living and the dead.

A little contingency planning, that doesn't even have to cost much either in time or money, can save your loved ones a lot of trouble and alleviate a lot of concerns. You owe them at least that much to make things as easy as possible on them. Let's hope it's all for nothing!

Reinventing Yourself

Life is full of things that we don't talk about because they are so fundamental that we take them for granted, like, where exactly does your electricity come from, or your water? Where exactly does your garbage go once the truck has picked it up? What actually happens to your euphemism after you've flushed it down the toilet?

Settled people take a lot of stuff for granted, and it could be argued, that living in cities is advantageous precisely because somebody, somewhere takes care of all this stuff; it's all somebody else's problem, which is what we pay our utilities bills and rates for.

It could also be argued that civilisation protects us a lot from our own stupidity and ignorance. We take paved roads for granted, if we get into trouble the police, ambulance and fire services are a phone call away. The list of things that we pay other people to handle is really large when you think about it – such is the life of the modern settled aristocrat.

But when you take up the nomadding life, these 'other' people all mysteriously disappear. All of a sudden, if you're in a remote location:

- The weather report isn't something that affects whether or not you're going to be inconvenienced, it could be a matter of life and death. See page 148 and 165.
- You just can't drop into a convenience store and pick up something that you've forgotten or go to the pharmacist and pick up a prescription that's slipped your mind.
- Emergency services might be a lot longer than the 20-minute average that you'd have to wait for an ambulance in Sydney – Australia's slowest response-time city.
- You have to have enough food, and especially, enough water to survive if you get into any difficulty in a really out of the way and hard to get to place.

- The waste that you produce, all has to go *somewhere*, and if you don't dispose of it properly, it
will end up attracting all sorts of unwanted attention – from wildlife to rangers.
- Leaving the lights on, or forgetting to turn off a tap, or turning it the wrong way, can have major repercussions.

Nomadding is supposed to be fun and satisfying. It's not supposed to degenerate into a desperate fight for survival. People die in the Australian outback from preventable causes all the time. These deaths don't usually make headlines because they're not sensational enough. Even more sobering, for every death there must be scores of near misses you never hear about. If you're going to put yourself out there, you need to leave your city self or even your country town self behind and reinvent yourself in more ways than one. You need to acquire some basic and some not so basic survival skills.

Staying Alive: Your Minimum Survival Skillset

At the very least, get a basic first aid certificate. Better, get an advanced first aid certificate. Better still, get a Statement of Attainment in Provide First Aid in Remote Situations. Shop around a bit for available courses. A minimum cost for a remote area basics two-day course is around $300 but there are longer courses available that cover more ground. It might be some of the best money you've ever spent. To get an idea of what you're in for you could contact 5 Star Training. Phone: 02 4722 2471
website: www.5startraining.com.au/courses/first-aid/remote-area-first-aid

If you plan to spend a lot of time reasonably close to population centres and not get too far off the beaten track, then the following advice might be overkill. But if you're more daring and adventurous and planning to go *way* off the beaten track, then there are a number of other courses that you might like to think about taking, which would be well worth the investment. Typical examples are:

- Bushcraft survival courses: here the emphasis is on staying alive.
- Wild foraging, wild edibles and fungi: take advantage of the wealth of bush food around you once you know how to identify it and prepare it.
- Survival technology skills: if you really want to 'go native' there are a number of low-tech survival tools you can learn to make. Our ancestors and Indigenous Australians used this stuff for thousands of years. This is an opportunity for old dogs to learn old tricks.
- Wilderness tracking and navigation: in other words, how not to get lost courses.

There are a number of reputable businesses all over the country offering bush survival courses. Here's a short list of examples that's by no means exhaustive:

- Australian Survival Instructors; Phone: 0423 572 048; **website: www.aussiesurvivalinstructors.com**
- Bush Lore Australia; Phone: 0409 885 949; **website: www.bushloreaustralia.com.au**
- Bushcraft Survival Australia; Phone: 0417 693 904; **website: www.bushcraftsurvivalaustralia.com.au**

There are also a number of websites that are full of information, like **www.survival.org.au**

But perhaps the most essential 'survival skills' that you can acquire in the modern era are how to use computers, tablets and mobile phones. Getting even a little techy can open up a whole world of information and broaden your options hugely. Modern technology doesn't have to be intimidating or frustrating. Any course that will get you started on basic information technology skills will put you well on the way to working out everything else. Go to page 193 for a special section that has all this covered.

The Survival Mindset

They say that a little knowledge is a dangerous thing, but when it comes to surviving in the Australian bush and the outback every little piece of knowledge helps. Most survival courses emphasise that in the more extreme cases it takes emergency services about three days to find you and get help to you. So if you can survive for three days then you stand a good chance of making it, even in the worst conditions. If you can survive longer, better still. So the more you know the better off you'll be.

It pays to know as much as you can but the most important thing that you can learn is the survival mindset. In short, having a survival mindset is like suddenly being able to go into an entirely different way of looking at the world and thinking, 'OK. We're in a bit of trouble here, but we have options. We know what we can do and even though we're still cautious, we're not overwhelmed. We can deal with this and we will pull through.'

Obviously, that sort of calm confidence doesn't come instantly, but if you take the time to learn about essential skills like fire lighting, emergency shelter construction, foraging for food, purifying water, celestial navigation and, hugely important, emergency signalling, there's no reason to end up a casualty, and every reason to have some amazing (if perhaps slightly exaggerated) survival stories to tell your grandchildren.

Staying Healthy

The vast majority of the time, we hope, grey nomadding will not be a desperate struggle for survival but a satisfying lifestyle change, filled with fun and adventure, even if sometimes it's adventure on a budget. But many a billionaire will tell you all the money in the world is no good to you if you're sick, and even those on modest means can have a great life if they're healthy, so staying healthy should be your number-one priority. Whole libraries are devoted to human health but here is a short summary of the things you need to keep in mind.

Diet

If you've been living in your body for several decades at least you should know by now what works for you and what doesn't. Some people thrive on vegetarianism, some suffer severe health problems unless they have some meat in their diet. Today, more and more people are getting used to the idea that many of us have to modify what we take into our bodies in order to stay healthy. Everyone is different. If there was an ideal, one-size-fits-all diet for everyone on the planet, surely, we would have found it by now. News flash! There isn't. Nevertheless, there are some basic principles that seem to work for most of us.

Eat plenty of fruit and vegetables. Contrary to popular belief fresh isn't always best, which is just as well, as in more remote regions it can be hard to find fresh vegetables. Frozen vegetables are often picked at their peak before being frozen and freezing has no effect on nutritional value. There are other surprises too. Corn begins to turn its sweet, easily digestible sugars into blander and harder-to-digest starches the very second that it's picked. Freezing arrests this process so in the case of corn the frozen product, believe it or not, is actually superior to fresh corn. Stocking up on frozen vegetables, if you have the freezer space, is not a bad idea, especially if they're on sale.

Drink plenty of water. Tea, coffee and alcohol actually encourage you to go to the toilet so water still is the best hydrator out there. If you really can't stand the taste of plain water, then start acquiring a taste for herbal teas. If you can get water filtration set up in your RV, that's an excellent investment, especially since bottled water is expensive and the quality of tap water varies hugely throughout the country.

Make sure you get enough vitamin C. Humans have to have vitamin C and unfortunately a nomadic diet can be lacking in

This is a picture from the farmers' markets, they are held all over Australia and one of the best places to try and find local food and produce.

it, unless you happen to know of some good bushfood sources. In fact, don't ignore any vitamin. The outback diet might not always provide optimal nutrition, especially if you find yourself eating a lot of takeaway food, and while multivitamin tablets might be overkill for most city dwellers, they can be a really good idea for nomads.

Eat as varied a diet as possible. Allowing for the exceptions created by food allergies, sensitivities and other problems, when it comes to food, variety is the best policy. Australia is justly regarded as having some of the best produce in the world so travelling is a fantastic premise for trying out things you might never have considered before. Take a walk on the culinary wild side and live a little.

And don't forget the potential delights of bush foods. As an excellent introduction to the under-explored world of Australian bush foods and their potential to promote human health, we recommend reading *Wild Foods* by Vic Cherikoff (**www.au.newhollandpublishers.com/wild-foods-2165.html**).

Catering for Special Diets

Those of us on special diets or who have a loved one who has dietary restrictions, for whatever reason, are all too aware of how much of a pain it can be getting the right supplies. But don't despair. We've found that local markets and local growers are the best solutions. You'd be surprised how many local markets there are around Australia. Once again, FRC has you covered and has created a continually updated list of them. Farm-gate trails are also becoming increasingly popular, and they're a real hit with nomads rocking into town and wanting to explore an area. The farm trail allows you to find small carts at the front of people's properties where you can not only find fresh home-grown vegies, often organic, or at least spray free, and, for a fraction of the cost of organics in shops. Failing all this, if there are food items you know that you can't get easily, you can bulk buy, or organise for them to be sent to you.

Exercise

The grey nomad lifestyle lends itself to about as much physical activity as you can stand. Living in an RV requires physical exertion. Even the RVs that you can control at the push of a button still require that you to do a lot. If that's not enough then there's no end to the walking, running and swimming opportunities that an outdoorsy nomadic lifestyle can offer. Of course some people do spend an inordinate amount of time in their foldable chairs doing nothing but swigging beers from a seemingly bottomless esky, so the outdoors don't automatically lend themselves to physical activity. And when the outdoors decides to conspire against you, and you find yourself effectively trapped in your RV while the rain pelts down for days on end, it's quite likely that you're going to spend a lot of time lying in bed, watching sports or reruns of *Seinfeld*. Nomadding isn't automatically a physically active life; the big difference is that exercise is part of the way of living, rather than a separate thing you do, say, at a gym.

One thing that you might like to do if you're staying at a site for any length of time is to set up an informal, regular exercise session with some new friends. While you might not be tempted to exercise much on your own, when you have other people joining in it's a strong motivator. Concentrate on bodyweight exercises that require no equipment and focus on flexibility too. All this stuff is great for keeping up bone density.

Medication

A study published online in the *Medical Journal of Australia* in January 2012 'A national census of medicines use: a 24-hour snapshot of Australians aged 50 years and older' reported that 87.1 per cent of respondents took one or more regular medications and in a 24-hour timeframe, 43.3 per cent had taken at least one medication. Overwhelmingly, the majority of older Australians are on something, the most common somethings being some form of blood pressure medication, anti-coagulants and agents for lowering lipids and for treating gastric reflux.

How you deal with keeping yourself supplied with medication is obviously a personal matter you have to work out on a case-by-case basis, but in general:

- Be organised. Don't lose track of your scripts.
- Be well supplied. Explain your lifestyle to you doctor so that you can be sure that you have enough of what you need, and then some extra in case of some sort of incident that compromises your supply.
- Stay on top of use-by dates. They are there for a reason and medication outside of use-by dates might not only be useless, they might cause harm.
- Store medicines strictly in accordance with the manufacturer's instructions. You might need insulated storage so that your medications aren't exposed to extremes of heat or moisture. Improper storage of medications can render them either ineffective or dangerous.

- Stay disciplined. Put some sort of system in place so that you don't 'forget' to take your medication. You might be able to get away with sloppiness in town but in the bush, you can't afford to allow your health management to slip.

FRC compiles a list of medical services, including doctors, pharmacies and allied health professionals. As the list grows nomads will be able to find help no matter where they are. In addition, nomads have the option to register to have their confidential medical records accessible to medical professionals no matter where they are under the Medicare My Health Record system.

Mental Health and Stress Management

Mental health is something that people take for granted until something happens, and it's then that you realise how disruptive and upsetting it is to have to deal with mental and emotional disturbances, including supporting someone close to you who has to deal with them.

It also comes as a surprise to many that nomadding is not a stress-free life but a life of different stresses. Just because you coped with a plethora of stresses in settled life doesn't mean that you'll automatically cope with the stresses of nomadic life. Remember that you probably spent decades adapting to your stressors both consciously and sub-consciously until you hardly think about your coping mechanisms anymore. But now you're playing a new game. It's going to take you a while to adjust and some of us take longer to adjust than others.

As far as stress management is concerned this is highly subjective and deeply personal. Some people deal with stress through physical activity and find mental activity enervating and vice versa. However, if there's one principle of keeping yourself mentally and emotionally healthy it's that of building and maintaining a strong social network.

Having said all this, time and time again you'll hear from nomads that, overall, the lifestyle helps you cope with stress a lot better than most. It might have something to do with being out in nature, days

You'll often need to do a lot of walking and climbing before you get to see views like this. Who needs a gym? Seriously!

full of positive, playful, life-affirming events, and all that fresh air, but this is just a theory.

Happy Hour

You might find that happy hour is one of the biggest stress relievers while on the road. It's part of the RV culture that usually, from about 4 pm to 6 pm each afternoon, around someone's campsite or campfire, somehow a few drinks and happy chatter just happen. Many find that happy hour is the best stress relief out there and nomads often find that simply telling a good yarn and having a great laugh puts them in a different frame of mind. And happy hour is also a great way to retell any disaster story that you might have as a funny anecdote to entertain your friends.

Mind you, you can still get the grumpy old campers that know it all and are still angry with the rest of the world.

Camping doesn't mean abandoning all your creature comforts.

You can almost gauge how long they have been on the road by their levels of pent-up rage, but usually after about six months or so, even the grumpiest of old campers will mellow. And if you do happen to be one of them, then yes, there is hope for you after a few months of intensive, nomadding therapy that includes a generous prescription of happy hours to be taken as often as needed.

Staying Connected

Connection – maintaining your relationships – is going to be harder when you're on the road than when you were living in one place all the time. It's important to know if you're a social introvert or a social extrovert. At the extremes, some people just don't need other people very much while others can't stand being alone. You probably know who you are but living your new life might lead you to re-examine the sort of person you thought you were. You might find that you need people less than you thought you did. You might find that you need people more.

Keeping Your Old Friends
Whether you're a social introvert or a social extrovert it's important that you don't lose touch with the people who are important to you. If you have to, make notes in a diary to remind yourself to touch base with your people. It's going to be easier for you to find them than it is for them to find you, so the first move is usually going to have to be yours. And remember that just because your schedule is now super-flexible doesn't mean theirs is, and just because you have all the time in the world doesn't mean that they do, so remember that no matter how much somebody loves you, it doesn't mean that they're free to talk when you are, or for as long as you can.

Staying healthy can be as simple as being limber enough to be able to sit down on a jetty and let your feet dangle in the water

Here is where social media can help a great deal, so if you don't know how to use it, take the time to learn. But remember that social media is only as good as you make it, and it's a supplement, not a substitute, for real connection.

Making New Friends

And much as you might love your old cronies the life of the nomad is full of opportunities for meeting new people, some of whom might become acquaintances, or even friends. Making and keeping friends as a nomad is the same as friendships among the settlers and in an age of mobile phones, emails and social media it's easier than ever to

Stress relief 101: There are worse ways of spending your time than simply sitting and watching the world go by.

keep in touch. The cautions are the same too. People aren't always how they present themselves and first impressions can be deceiving, for good or bad. You need to be the judge of how you conduct your relationships – what you like and what you don't like, what you will or won't put up with. It's also easier to run away when you're a nomad, for good or ill. However, be aware that though they're spread out across the country, if you're out there long enough you begin to realise that the grey nomad community is a part of the community of regular campers and that that community is really just a big country town, again, for good and bad. People know things, or *think* they know things, word spreads, both truth and lies. The take home message here is that the social and practical support you get from the community as a whole and your capacity to make and keep friends, will depend on your social skills, and your reputation is key.

Remember that you'll be moving into a space the size of your bathroom. If your wardrobe looks anything like this, you'll have some serious downsizing to do.

Psychological Adjustments

There are a host of psychological adjustments that you're going to have to make if you're going to make a success of being a nomad. These adjustments tend to come in two stages, although there's no clear boundary between one and the other: leaving it all behind and adapting to being there.

Leaving It All Behind

Exchanging one way of life for another isn't just about saying 'hello' to your new life, it's about saying 'goodbye' to your old one.

Say goodbye to a lot of your stuff. This, of course, depends on whether you keep your current home, which then becomes a storage facility, or you sell up everything. So at the sell-up extreme you're going to be giving away, selling or throwing out the vast majority of your material possessions. You don't need to watch the reality TV shows about decluttering to tell you how difficult this is for some people. Find a celebrity declutterer whose method works for you or find a ruthless friend. This is decluttering on steroids and you might need to do it in stages. Some tips include:

- Don't burden your friends with things they don't want.
- Don't present your junk to people as gifts, give them the option to politely refuse.
- Don't burden people with 'permanent loans', giving you the option of taking things back when you want them. Your friends are not your cheap storage locker. Either keep the thing or cut the umbilical cord.

Say goodbye to your friends and family. Unlike your things this isn't a permanent goodbye, but this is like taking a very long trip with no end in sight.

Say goodbye to old ways of doing things. The way you wash, launder, eat, dress and entertain yourself will all need to be revised. Don't underestimate how disrupting these multiple changes, big and small will be.

Adapting to Being There

You're going to have to get used to living in a more confined space, with a lot less stuff than you're used to. Even the biggest and most elaborate of rigs is small compared to even a small house. The physical adjustment can be somewhat eased through good design that suits you and the way you like to live (page 115) but there will still be the mental and psychological adjustment of living in a more confined space. This is why we recommend that if you can, you should rent some sort of rig, similar to the one you plan to live in long-term, so that you can identify what works for you and what doesn't. Pay particular attention to what really annoys you, as it tends not to be the big things that do people in, but little things that just keep picking at you day after day after day.

You're going to have to get used to living outdoors. Even if you're already an outdoorsy type person you're going to up the ante on outdoor living when you go nomad. Your sense of space will expand, your sense of personal distance too. That invisible perimeter that you don't even think about, that circle around you that acts as the boundary between 'close' and 'too close' might shift. You might also see the boundary between inside and outside blurring. This might not be noticeable to you, but your settled friends might notice it when you come to visit.

You are going to become much more self-reliant and your learning curve will sometimes seem like a vertical cliff. If you've let years go by without learning anything new you might need to relearn how to learn.

You're going to be doing a lot of driving, or driver support. Unless you're a professional driver who's used to being on the road all the time, you'll find yourself doing more driving, under more diverse conditions, than ever before. This is fatiguing, and you're going to have to put things in place so that fatigue or bad judgement, doesn't cause accidents (page 181).

Renegotiating Your Relationships

Since human beings are social animals our relationships with each other are crucial to our survival. Since you're recalibrating your life, you'll want the transition to be as smooth as possible. This means preparing for the most common comments and objections that people in your life might raise in response to your major change.

Breaking the News to Your Family and Friends

This doesn't have to be hard. Depending on your personality, you might just blurt it all out or have some sort of announcement prepared. Depending on your friends and family, you're going to get everything from supportive acceptance to what seems like a third-degree interrogation.

Supportive acceptance is easy, interrogation might go easier on you if, like a politician at a press conference, you anticipate some of the questions, and you have answers prepared.

Common Objections from Your Kids

Q: When will we see you?

A: Whenever we're in town. Whenever we decide to. We'll make a special effort for birthdays. There's nothing stopping you from meeting us in the middle somewhere.

Q: What are we going to do about babysitting?

A: Do what everyone else does. Either pay a responsible teenager or have some sort of babysitting exchange with your friends.

Q: But your grandkids will miss you.

A: We're travelling, we're not dying. We're sure that they'll be fine.

Q: Why are you frittering away our inheritance?

A: We're not frittering away anything. It's our money and we're choosing to spend it like this. If we've done our jobs as parents right,

That's right, son. We've spent your inheritance. Deal with it.

we've empowered you to look after yourselves rather than depend on some windfall after we die. We're sure you'll be fine.

Q: You won't last a month!

A: We've done our research. We've done a trial. We have a back-up plan if it all goes pear-shaped. Whether it lasts a month, a year, or a couple of decades this is how we want to spend our lives.

Q: What if you die on the road?

A: Didn't you hear us when we told you about our back-up plans? Part of the back-up if something major happens is appropriate provisions in the case of death. Here, we've put it all in a book for you (page 76). You'll be fine.

Common Objections from Your Friends

Q: When will we see you?

A: See answer above.

Q: You're abandoning us!

A: Nice try with the emotional blackmail, but no, we're not

abandoning anybody. We're just embracing a new way of living. You're welcome to join us if you like. We'll help you prepare. It'll be fun!

Q: You're being irresponsible!

A: To whom? To what? The kids are grown up. We're moving from being responsible for things we don't need to be responsible for, like a big house and all this stuff, and being responsible to and for ourselves.

The above answers should cover, in principle at least, the majority of cases. To drive home the point – no pun intended – it doesn't really matter what other people think. At the end of the day it is *your* journey, not someone else's. Yes, many people in your life will feel the need to put forward their views on how 'abnormal' your chosen lifestyle is, but that's simply because they don't understand it or haven't experienced it. Most people come around to acceptance, in time.

Remember, it'll probably take you a few months to settle into this new life too even though you're already in a positive frame of mind about it.

Your Relationship with Your Partner

This is a biggie. The reality of nomadding is that you're probably going to be spending more time with your partner than you have since your honeymoon phase. The close confines of an RV can turn into a pressure cooker, and no matter how much love there is in a relationship, if there's anything that you've swept under the carpet, put aside, ignored or not dealt with, *it will come up*.

This is where, if you haven't learned it already, you're going to have to get used to the idea that arguments can be healthy, that flexibility is not the same as martyring yourself, that compromise is not the same as compromising yourself and that you don't have to set yourself on fire to keep someone warm. This is when you're going to have to pick your battles and not sweat the small stuff.

Redrawing the Boundaries with Your Partner

Whatever arrangements you've negotiated over the years with your partner during your settled years, nomadding will necessitate a whole host of new agreements. The most important agreements that you'll have to come to are:

1. Personal space. People need to know that 'this is my space, this is your space, and this is our space'.

2. Being realistic. Knowing that when space is limited and resources are limited, space will inevitably be violated, even with the best of intentions. Some couples find themselves tested in odd ways. They might discover that circumstances will force them to go to the toilet in front of each other, especially if the weather is bad, or if someone gets sick. And, to be blunt, it's difficult to hide explosive diarrhoea in an RV.

3. Things that have to be joint responsibility out of sheer necessity. See page 181.

www.frc.camp/frustratingwife

The Top-Ten Reasons Couples Fight

In spite of people's general impression that they are unique, the same rubbish tends to play out in the majority of relationships. Probably because unless you had extremely enlightened and communicative parents or teachers and you were an attentive student, the majority of people aren't taught *how* to have relationships. They've usually done things by being exposed to (often bad) examples, or they've winged it and made a right mess of things. It helps if you know that your arguments with your partner are not special.

1. Accuracy of recollection. These are arguments that start when people have very different memories about what was said, by whom, to whom, about what, and what, if any, agreements were made. These are the arguments where someone is likely to say, 'Oh, if *only* I'd recorded that conversation.' Given that smartphones today come with the capacity to record, there's no excuse not to record conversations that might have major implications. It might seem weird at first, but it forces people to up their game and actually say what they really mean and stick to a promise if they make one.

2. Agendas. You might think that you're doing the same thing for the same reason. You might not be. Agendas aren't always deliberately hidden. Sometimes people aren't clear or don't communicate clearly about why they want something, even though they think they have.

3. Sometimes it's just innocent bad communication and misunderstanding. This leads to a 'Why are we in Goondiwindi?' conversation.

'OK, So, remind me again. Why are we in Goondiwindi?'

'I don't know. I thought you wanted to go to Goondiwindi.'

'I didn't want to go to Goondiwindi. I only wanted to come to Goondiwindi because I thought that you wanted to go to Goondiwindi.'

'I didn't want to go to Goondiwindi. I only wanted to go to Goondiwindi because I thought that you wanted to go to Goondiwindi.'

At this point either laughter or a heated argument ensues, depending on the current state of the relationship.

4. Cooking. 'I can't eat that.' 'I won't eat that.' 'Why are you the only person in the world who can burn water?' 'Why do I always have to do all the cooking and the washing up?'

5. Family. 'You've always hated my sister.' 'You've always thought my brother was a loser.' 'I really don't want to drive a thousand kilometres just to catch up with your stupid cousins.'

6. Interior design. 'I'm no expert but I really don't think the burnt amber curtains go with the lime green walls.' 'Why do you keep buying these knick-knacky pieces of crap?'

7. Money. This is so self-explanatory we're not even going to give an example.

8. Sex. Ditto. In serious cases both sex and money issues need the intervention of expert help.

9. The children. Don't think that just because they're out of sight, they're out of mind. Your children will continue to be a part of your lives wherever you happen to be nomadding. If you're still arguing about them after all these years then nomadding isn't going to change that.

10. Tidiness and cleaning. This is a major issue for several reasons: People confuse 'untidiness' with 'unclean'. The two are related, but not at all the same thing. You can have a perfectly clean things that are a mess, dirty stuff that looks ordered, or both. People's standards of what constitutes tidy or clean vary tremendously and even if people have similar standards, they'll only clean what they can see. Short people tend to ignore high places, tall people tend to ignore low places. Also, when dealing with a couple the 'clean freak' of the two ends up doing 'all the work' and can tend to be a bit of a martyr about it. And crucially, when you live in an RV every bit of dirt shows up, because while you can hide things in a larger space, a small space has no 'give'. For more about cleaning see page 206.

Who Gets the Blame?

The 'It's your fault' arguments can get ugly. The only way out of these is that people need to:

1. Negotiate who is responsible for what.
2. Honour those responsibilities.
3. Accept that when someone is responsible for something, the non-responsible party has very little right to criticise the responsible party. After all, if they could do a better job, maybe they should have taken a responsibility in the first place. It's all about drawing the line and establishing healthy boundaries.

Growing Together

One thing we hear time and time again is that, while nomadding couples might face a challenge or two on the way, they deal with these challenges together, as a team. The result is that couples find that they not only grow as individuals, but together. It's not that a pre-nomad life necessarily drives couples apart (although, to be frank, it often does), but when you factor in year after year of focusing on careers, mortgages, children and all sorts of other stuff attention is not necessarily on the couple.

You really are in this together. Heaven help you if you're not.

Nomadding provides opportunities for couples to make joint decisions about everything; in fact, they have to. And it's this process of constantly being aware that you're a team, that you're in this together, that makes nomadding couples some of the strongest couples around.

Your Relationship with Yourself

Libraries have been written about people taking on a new life and 'finding themselves'. The thing is, that the only way you find yourself is by putting yourself in all sorts of different situations and seeing how you deal with them. And because the number of potential situations you can find yourself in is infinite, self-discovery is an endless process. The major challenge is feeling that you're out of your depth, but this is only if you don't know what to do. The best way to keep a healthy relationship with yourself is to educate yourself continually about all the different aspects of your new life. With any luck all the research that you're doing will mean that you'll know what to do no matter what your new life throws at you, or at the very least, make a well-educated guess as to the right course of action.

Travelling Alone

This guidebook assumes that most grey nomads travel in pairs and, more rarely, as groups of friends, simply because that's the statistical reality. However, there are a substantial number of men and women who go it alone, and quite successfully too, both short-term and long-term. In fact, there are possibly more solo women out there than solo men and they usually go nomad as the result of a major life change.

Independent people usually know who they are, and they usually know what they can or can't do. But, to emphasise a repeating theme in this book, independence in a settled life is not the same as independence in a nomadding life. Life as a modern gypsy will make demands on you that you haven't had to meet before, and, most importantly, in many situations you'll have no-one to back you up or to help you. Of course, people who you encounter on your travels will be more than happy to help, but you can't rely on that. You can't *bet* on that. Solo nomads need to have as many tricks in their bag as their bag of tricks can hold.

The most important are:

- Basic medical knowledge and first aid
- Basic survival skills
- Basic mechanical skills
- Intermediate motoring skills
- Basic information technology skills

For some appropriate feistiness, go to:

www.frc.camp/angel

Isolation and Loneliness

Like 'dirty' and 'untidy', 'loneliness' and 'isolation' are related terms that don't mean the same thing. Isolation is about being separated from other people, physically, socially or both. Loneliness is a feeling that this separation is a problem. The repeated emphasis on being as skilled-up as possible is all about ensuring that you survive whatever nomadding throws at you when you are isolated. Loneliness is another matter, and it is about managing your emotions and your sense of connectedness to other people, if that is important to you. Curing loneliness is mostly a matter of finding like-minded or like-hearted people; people who 'get' you either mentally, emotionally or both. Loneliness tends to vanish when you are in the presence of others who make you feel good in their presence. There are plenty of opportunities for you to connect on a continent that has twenty-five million human inhabitants, and millions of animals you can make friends with too.

Going solo doesn't mean going solo all the time. Many solos join temporary convoys of other solos and share stories, experiences and skills along the way. This might be an especially attractive option to those who might occasionally get pangs of loneliness, no matter how independent they are.

Pets

According to the RSPCA, 62 per cent of Australian households have pets – one of the highest rates of pet ownership in the world. Pet 'owners' or 'carers' and their pets have a unique relationship and no two pets are alike.

Pet owners often worry if their pets will adapt to nomadding but like everything else, you can't be absolutely sure until you give it a try. Some take really well to travel as long as they're always in the proximity of their human. Some become neurotic messes. How well do you know your pet? Will they thrive or barely survive? Will they adapt or perish?

To many people's surprise you can teach an old dog, and an old cat, new tricks. In fact, many an older pet finds a new zest for living in a life of travel. Some pets, however, even with the best intentions, cannot adapt to nomadding. After all, nomadding is your decision, not *theirs*. It's important therefore that when it comes to your pets you have a 'plan B' if life on the road doesn't work out for Fido the dog or Mimsy the cat.

These things have to be handled with some delicacy. No family member or friend needs to feel that they're being lumped with your pet just because you've decided on the nomad life. You also need to accept that some pets will have a 'whatever' attitude to going to a new home, whereas others will have abandonment issues.

Even though there are millions of birds, reptiles, horses, rabbits, guinea pigs and other small mammal pets, by far the most common pets are dogs and cats, particularly when it comes to nomads, and they deserve a special mention. The information below is only a quick summary. Feel free to do further research. Your first stop could be **www.wideopenpets.com**

Dogs

In spite of the size of Australia and the popularity of dogs, you cannot assume that dogs will be welcome everywhere, particularly in caravan parks. It's vitally important then that if you're travelling with a dog, you know that you and Fido will have a place to stay. As a general rule, dogs (and cats) are *not* allowed in National Parks, even for day trips. However, State Forests have different rules so it's best to check ahead.

Even in places where dogs can go, they might not be allowed off their lead. Fido might find that he has even less freedom than if you had stayed in the burbs. In this case, having good current knowledge about where you can take Fido is vital, which is why having access to FRC Premium Membership (page 314 to 318) is such a good idea.

FRC has an ongoing development program of a register of pet shelters, pet sitters and vets to assist you if you need someone to look after your furbaby as well as pet insurance if you need it. See also:

www.frc.camp/travelwithpets

and

www.frc.camp/3dogs1bird

At a more mundane level, some people love having a very cuddly relationship with their dogs, others prefer a little distance.

Having a dog in an RV boils down to one question: Can you put up with the smell of wet dog in a campervan or trailer for days at a time?

You'll also need to make space for your furbaby. This includes bedding and storage for food and other basics. The same adaptations to minimalism you have to make for yourself apply to your pets too. There simply isn't enough room for more than a couple of leads (one spare if the main one breaks) or for more than one dog tent. It's unlikely that there will to be room for twenty different toys. In any case, with an entire continent to explore, most dogs will be in heaven, sniffing about all over the place. As is the case with your partner, you'll probably find that you'll be spending a lot more time with your dog as a nomad than you ever did in your regular life. Many people report getting pangs of guilt when they realise how much they might have been neglecting Fido and also realise that Fido has actually gotten thinner, fitter, psychologically and physically healthier since they started nomadding. Perhaps this is because dogs are just domesticated wolves and wolves are natural nomads anyway.

Separation Anxiety

No matter how much you love your furbabies, there will inevitably be times when you'll have to leave them alone for a bit. You might have to zip down to the shops or you might have to put them in a kennel for a few days while you go on an adventure that isn't dog or cat friendly and you won't be able to organise a sitter. Cats generally handle separation better than dogs, but not all dogs are the same. Just in case you didn't know, some dog breeds are more susceptible to separation anxiety than others. If you don't have a dog yet, and if you're thinking about getting one, check with your vet about how a particular dog breed generally handles separation anxiety.

Cats and Others

Anecdotally, cats tend to adapt surprising well to nomadding. Whereas dogs are generally happy if they're with their pack, cats tend to adopt a particular favourite human and as long as that human is reasonably available they're OK. You can leave them alone or with a friend for long periods of time. This might or might not be a problem; it depends on the cat. Cats have various ways of making their various displeasures known.

Never leave a dog or a cat inside an RV for any length of time. If anything happens to you and you're delayed, your pet will be in serious trouble. Besides, leaving a pet in a vehicle for longer than a reasonable period of time constitutes animal abuse and if anyone finds out you could be in serious trouble.

A quick word about domestic cats and wildlife. Whereas dogs are domestic, cats are still somewhat wild animals that are barely tamed. They are hunters – built to hunt and they like it too. Responsible cat custodianship means monitoring your cat so that it doesn't go off wandering somewhere, rendering the local wildlife one kill closer to extinction.

Consider perhaps acquiring an outdoor pen for your cat if you have to leave kitty alone for any period of time. Consider also that cats are nocturnal, and might be more active at night when you want to sleep in the confines of your RV.

There are, therefore, some nomadding cat essentials that will take some of your valuable space:
- Cat carrier
- Portable litter box
- Portable outdoor cat fence/tent
- Catch scratcher
- Cat toys
- Collapsible indoor/outdoor cat house
- Odour-masking kitty litter
- Collapsible food and water bowls
- Leash and harness
- Airtight food storage
- Window perch

(Source: www.rvblogger.com/blog/rv-with-cataccessories – retrieved 07/10/2019.)

Also, a quick word about birds. Birds are increasingly popular pets among nomads but be warned, the same restrictions that apply to dogs and cats also apply to birds and access to national parks.

Pet Etiquette

As difficult as it might be for animal lovers to imagine, some people just don't like dogs or cats. Many pet owners automatically assume that other people are going to love their pets. Many pets assume that everyone is going to love them too. These are dangerous assumptions, so be mindful if your dog (it's usually a dog) trespasses on somebody else's personal space. On the other side of the equation, if you don't like other people's pets you should be firm but clear about it. If the pet owner is so clueless that they don't take the hint they have no right to be shocked if you decide to be, say, more assertive about how much you don't want Fido to pester you.

Basic Pet Checklist

Before you take your pets on any long journey, or a total change of life, keep the following things in mind.

- Book a visit to the vet. Give your pet a health check just to make sure that there aren't any problems that might cause complications later.
- Campsite selection. Make absolutely sure if you're going to a campsite or to a national park that they don't have a problem with pets, especially dogs. Phone ahead first if you have to.
- Documentation and medication. Make sure that licences, ID tags, vaccinations and flea and tick treatments are current and that computer tag chips are in working order.
- First aid. Pets need a first aid kit just as much as humans do. Make sure that yours is fully stocked for your specific pet and that you know basic pet first aid. Domestic pets aren't used to the wilds and they can get into trouble particularly from ticks and snakes.
- Leash, tether, stake. If you have a leash, tether and stake arrangement you can stake your dog with plenty of wiggle room so that you don't have to be constantly holding the leash.

- Poop bags. Just because you're in the middle of the bush doesn't mean that you don't need to pick up after your dog. Toilet hygiene is important at many campsites and in many parks too in order to keep trails clean.
- Sleeping arrangements. If, for whatever reason the RV is unavailable where is your pet going to sleep? Is your cat going to snuggle up with you in a tent? Does your dog have their own kennel tent or shade tent? If not, as we've already hinted, we highly recommend that you acquire one as there are sure to be days when you'll regret *not* getting one.

There are many places where pets aren't allowed, but there are many where they are. After all is said and done, nomads often discover that their furbabies not only adjust to life on the road, they have the time of their lives.

This dog goes camping with his own tent.

This couple travel with three dogs.

... and this Kookaburra travels alone, but might want to share part of its journey with you.

PART THREE

THE RIG

///

Choosing Your Vehicle

If there is one thing that will determine the quality of your grey nomad experience more than any other it's the sort of vehicle or arrangement of vehicles, that you'll be travelling in – the rig. At the very minimum, a light-travelling, sol o grey nomad's rig will consist of a motorbike and whatever the nomad can carry in a backpack; at the maximum the rig can be a state-of-the-art, expedition-quality mobile transport that can set you back over a million dollars – and everything in between.

Rigs come in many types, shapes, sizes and configurations – more about the specifics later – but unless you're already living in a tiny house and you're going to be upgrading to a military transport that you can take to Antarctica, then the overwhelming likelihood is that you'll be moving into a space that's a lot smaller than the space that you're used to living in.

Imagine Moving into Your Bathroom

Australians have the largest houses in the world, with an *average* usable floor space of 214 square metres (2300 square feet). This is an average, which means that many Australians live in spaces that are even bigger. This average size even tops the United States (at 201 square metres or 2163 square feet). Compare this to the United Kingdom (at 76 square metres or 820 square feet) and you can see that Australians are used to livin' large – larger than anyone else on the planet.

Now put this into context when you realise that even the *largest* average RV (recreational vehicle) is 40 square metres (430 square feet), and those are *outside* dimensions. Round those figures off and suddenly it becomes clear that even if you get a very large RV, you're effectively losing 80 per cent of your living space. It therefore takes significant physical, mechanical and psychological adjustment to become an RV-living nomad if you're used to larger living spaces. You just won't have anywhere near the space you're used to especially since RVs are generally even smaller than 40 square metres – think more like 20 or even 10. At this point moving into your mobile home really does become like moving into your bathroom.

So, what exactly are your options?

Recreational Vehicles: An Overview

Even though nomads think of their rigs as homes, the manufacturers of RVs never *originally* envisaged their vehicles as permanent long-term dwellings. Of course, with the rise of the grey nomad and people seeking alternatives to the conventional lifestyle, and with improvements in technology, the RV landscape has changed somewhat, but 'recreational vehicle' seems to be a term that we're stuck with, so we'll work with that.

RVs come in several basic forms, each with their advantages and disadvantages. However, you should note some realities that affect all RVs, regardless of their configuration or style.

- They are not houses. They are not buildings. A house is generally designed to deal with a fixed and at least somewhat predictable climate that undergoes a regular seasonal cycle. The Queensland bungalow is, by definition, different to a Victorian terrace. The very nature of nomadding means that your RV is going to be exposed to a far broader range of climatic and environmental conditions than any fixed dwelling. Some RVs handle these environmental changes better than others.

- Their greatest strength – mobility – is their greatest weakness. Depending on how often you're on the road, and for how long, you're RV is going to be exposed to stresses and forces that are the equivalent of exposing a house to regular earth tremors. Of course, they are built for this, but these stresses, the inevitable damage and wear and tear, will determine how long your RV lasts and in what condition.

Maintenance is therefore vital.

How Long Will an RV Last?

The following estimates assume that you're using a motorhome, but they can also give you a rough guide as to the longevity of towable RVs. How long can you expect your RV to last? The short answer is twenty years, or 320,000 kilometres (200,000 miles), whichever comes first. However, several factors come into play.

- How often you travel. Every time you set up and set down that's more wear and tear.

- The conditions that you expose your RV to, including climatic extremes, terrain, road conditions and saltwater. You should

note that even arid regions in Australia can be quite salty so 'saltwater' isn't necessarily a coastal issue.
- How much weight you're regularly carrying. Are you travelling light, or are you always near the maximum load?
- How quickly you attend to repairs – the 'stitch in time saves nine' principle.
- How good your maintenance is and how regularly you perform it.
- How well you store your RV when it's not in use if intermittent home-base dwelling is part of the way that you've arranged things for yourselves.

The big lesson here is that like everything else, the better you treat it the longer it's going to last. The way you interact with your RV on a day-to-day basis will be a major factor in the longevity of your RV. Treat your vehicle with respect, give it what it needs and prepare it properly for what you will be demanding of it. Do all that and there's every reason to believe that your RV will last longer than the usual twenty-year life.

A Note About Licences

In spite of their size, for most motorhomes no special licence is required to drive one. This isn't always the case, so if your heart is set on a particular motorhome that does require a special licence, you are going to have to factor in the time and cost of acquiring one as well as the skills to drive it.

Even without a special driving licence, the ordinary one that you have must be a full licence, not a provisional one and the license holder must be below the age of seventy-five to drive an RV after which time a medical assessment is required each year. If you're renting an RV, and the licence holder is between seventy and seventy-five then additional paperwork and insurance is generally required.

For further information, go to:

www.roadsafety.transport.nsw.gov.au/stayingsafe/ontheroad-65plus/licences.html

Motorhomes – Class A

At least the term 'motorhome' makes a concession to the possibility that someone might choose to make a vehicle a permanent dwelling. Motorhomes are the largest RVs. They are fully integrated, one-piece units. The largest motorhomes, known as 'Class As', are about 2.9 metres in width (9.5 feet) and 13.7 metres long (45 feet), at least in the United States. Australian vehicles are limited to being 2.5 metres (8.2 feet) before they become classified as 'wide loads' and require special permits to be on the road. There are also smaller Class Cs and Class Bs, although, funnily enough, the Class Cs are larger than the Class Bs. Class Bs are often referred to as campervans, so see below for more on the Class Bs and Class Cs.

Motorhomes can run on petrol or diesel, and some are now available that run on LPG or have LPG as a backup. The main advantage of diesel is that they require less maintenance, fewer things can go wrong with a diesel engine and they have more torque.

It's almost inconceivable that you'd want to take a large vehicle on the road without roadside assistance insurance such as that offered by organisations like the NRMA (page 170). However, be aware that even NRMA premium coverage only covers towing up to 100 kilometres and vehicles under 10 tonnes, so if you're going to go big make sure that you take out extra insurance that covers the size of your vehicle. It may pay to look at other options, including the Let's Go Caravan Insurance policy offered by FRC, which provides complimentary prestige upgrades for their Premium Club Members.

The RV market is dominated by US manufacturers, but there are many excellent Australian manufacturers too. There are strict guidelines for RVs in Australia but for a precise idea of what is allowable on Australian roads either talk to the dealers and manufacturers themselves or find comprehensive resources at the National Heavy Vehicle Register at:

www.nhvr.gov.au/road-access/mass-dimension-and-loading/
general-mass-and-dimension-limits

Advantages

Class A motorhomes have the largest interior space of any RVs. Additionally, some models incorporate slide-out sections that expand the interior space even more. If you're caught in inclement weather for a long time, you'll appreciate every little extra square inch.

There are plenty of options available in finishes, configurations, layouts, decoration and customisation. If you love your creature comforts, a Class A motorhome might be your only realistic, long-term, nomadic living solution.

They lend themselves to off-grid living because there's plenty of room on the roof for solar panels and there's a lot of room for storage, particularly water, petrol and gas.

Disadvantages

Some people find the motorhome's size, especially the Class A's, to be intimidating – not only to maintain but to drive too. If you've only driven small cars all your life then driving a bus-sized motorhome might take a little getting used to.

Unlike smaller vehicles that you might be able to take anywhere, driving a motorhome is a bit like lugging a small house around. Day trips are hard to make unless you're either towing or driving an auxiliary vehicle. This doesn't bother some people who have motorbikes secured to their motorhomes, and in some cases, people do have either a convoy or a towed configuration consisting of a motorhome and a four-wheel drive. They leave the motorhome behind at a secure location use the 4WD for their short-stay trips or journeys into more rugged locations, where no other vehicle can or is allowed to go.

Motorhomes in general, but especially the bigger Class As, are expensive, and in more ways than one. Top-of-the-range motorhomes can easily start at $250,000 and, if importing some American models converted to Australian conditions, then the really big ones can set you back easily in the $750,000 range. Some of the more modest Class Cs hover at around $150,000 and the Class Bs might be as low as in the $60,000 to $80,000 range.

They are also expensive to maintain. The larger motorhomes might require a Medium Rigid licence, so you have to factor the time and expense to acquire one into your up-front costs. Then there's also:

• Registration, including compulsory third-party insurance.
• Insurance, from basic to comprehensive.
• Fuel costs, which, when you're lugging around a vehicle in the range of 10 tonnes, can add up.
• Other maintenance and operational costs such as servicing.
• Repair costs. Not every garage is equipped to repair these babies and getting spare parts might be a bit of a headache too.

Class A Approximate Maximum Dimensions
- Width: 2.5 metres (8.2 feet)
- Length: 6.4 to 13.7 metres (21 to 45 feet)
- Height: 3 metres (10 feet)
- Weight: 15 tonnes to 18 tonnes (33,000 to 40,000 pounds)

The Class As are as close to a palace on wheels as most mortals are likely to experience … with interiors to match.

Motorhomes Class B – the Campervan

The campervan is the smallest of the integrated, self-contained motorhomes. As its name implies it's built on a van chassis and, although that chassis can range from the size of a small delivery van, most commercial models are in the larger van size range. Being vans, the commercial ones tend to look sleek and compact.

Advantages
- Their size makes them easy to handle, drive and set up at a campsite.
- They are still expensive, compared to cars, but much cheaper to run, maintain and repair than Class As and Class Cs.

- They're small enough that daytrips and excursions are a no-brainer.
- A well-designed campervan will give you access to the basic amenities that make life comfortable including: heating and air conditioning, refrigeration, hot water, sink, showers (usually external), and a toilet.

Disadvantages
- Really limited interior space, which isn't necessarily a bad thing if you're travelling in good weather but can be really hellish if things get either too hot, too cold or too wet, or if there are biting insects around and you haven't made provision for them.
- Limited amenities. Yes, you can fit a small refrigerator and toilet in a campervan. Yes, you can have an *outdoor* shower, but forget about laundry facilities and, usually, indoor cooking.
- Inflexibility for guests. A campervan is best either for solo travel or for two people who *really* like each other. If you're planning on entertaining guests, they're going to have to bring along their own rig or tent.
- Very limited storage. Even a roof rack or towed trailer will only take you so far.
- Usually not powerful enough to tow a second vehicle but might be able to carry a small motorbike.

Class B Approximate Maximum Dimensions
- Width: 2.5 metres (8.2 feet)
- Length: 6 to 7.6 metres (20 to 25 feet)
- Height: 2.1 to 2.75 metres (7 to 9 feet)
- Weight: 4.5 tonnes to 9 tonnes (10,000 to 20,000 pounds)

The campervan is, versatile, neat and compact. Perhaps a little too compact for some.

But if you're a compact person ... you don't have to sacrifice space for comfort.

Motorhomes Class C

The Class Cs sit in the goldilocks zone of RVs for many people being neither mobile-palace Class As nor the Class Bs that are more suited to singles or couples (at a stretch). They are built on a truck chassis and typically have an extension built over the main driving cabin that usually has a 'loft' sleeping or storage area. They tend to look boxy, rather than aerodynamic but they're built for comfort, practicality and endurance, not for speed.

Advantages
- Self-contained with all the basic necessities.
- Have many of the advantages of Class As but with much lower purchase, maintenance and running costs.
- Large enough for families.
- Versatile.

Disadvantages
- Expensive to maintain and operate for many.
- Require better-than-basic driving skills.
- Not as basic as a Class B but still has to be a bit skimpy on luxury because of lack of space. Nevertheless, some of the newer models have surprising, creature-comfort features.

Class C Approximate Maximum Dimensions
- Width: 2.5 metres (8.2 feet)
- Length: 8.5 metres (28 feet)
- Height: 3 metres (10 feet)
- Weight: 9 tonnes to 13.6 tonnes (20,000 to 30,000 pounds)

Towable RVs

The great advantage of the towable RVs is that they separate the motoring functions from the living functions. The result is a home that can't go anywhere under its own power, and reversing can be

The Class Cs are, for many grey nomads, the right compromise between size and versatility ...

very challenging. However, reversing becomes easier with a bit of practice and helpful devices such as caravan movers can assist a lot with manoeuvring.

In spite of some minuses, this sort of rig does leave you with a detachable vehicle that you can use for day trips and short camps. To many, the towable RV's flexibility is what makes it attractive, but there are a few things to consider that are universal to all towables.

The towing vehicle itself has to be powerful enough to pull the *full load;* not just an empty RV, but an RV full of all the stuff that you're taking, including the maximum number of people that you could conceivably take. 'Load' includes having to pull the towable up and down inclines. 'Load' also includes a wide range of road conditions from 'ideal, dry and paved to borderline impassable, bogged-down, muddy messes. Your vehicle should have the best fuel economy that you can get and easy maintenance and repair are always bonuses.

Towing is a driving skillset all on its own and requires learning new techniques and lots of practice. We suggest doing a course to gain some invaluable skills the easy way, rather than throwing yourself in at the deep end and committing some expensive mistakes. Towing courses are available throughout the country and the list below is just a brief guideline. If they can't help you, maybe they can recommend someone who can. Courses generally run in the $300 to $400 range for a day course. That isn't charged per person but covers one RV rig, so couples are encouraged to attend. Some examples include:

- NSW: Tow-Ed Penrith; phone 1300 605 660.
- QLD: Learn 2 Tow Elanora; phone 0418 265 674.
- VIC: METEC Bayswater North; phone 03 9725 4758.

For further information go to:

www.withoutahitch.com.au/caravan/best-caravan
-driving-courses-australia

... and that bit of extra space above the cabin comes in very handy.

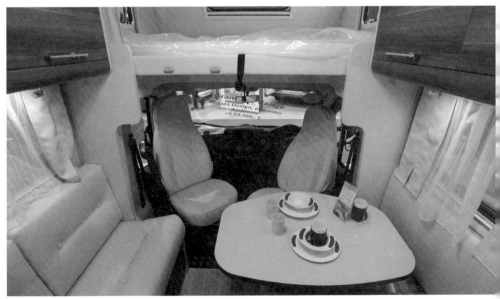

An Important Point About Weight

One of the things many people don't realise with caravans in Australia is that, on average, once you consider weight limitations, caravans can leave you with a budget of only about 400 kilograms (1000 pounds) to put in your belongings. Take away about 100 kilograms for water this leaves about 300 kilograms (750 pounds) for clothing and belongings. The vast majority of people will exceed this easily, so once again, you're going to have to embrace minimalism. There are portable caravan scales that can be used to weigh caravans, just to be sure, or you can go over a weigh bridge from time to time to check how you're doing.

Caravans, Travel Trailers and Camper Trailers

These are probably the first thing that comes to mind when you think towable RVs. The range, size and quality are huge, from compact basic to elaborate, multi-axeled, state of the art. The range of shapes is surprising, from the smaller, aerodynamic teardrops to box-like houses on wheels. They are much less expensive than motorhomes of equivalent sizes (sometimes half the cost), but you have to factor in the cost of your towing vehicle, that can range anywhere from $50,000 to $150,000.

Fifth Wheels

This is a variation on the caravan/trailer theme that has a 'goose neck' extension that overhangs the back of a utility vehicle. There are a number of advantages to this arrangement.

- It provides a much better connection to the towing vehicle.
- The gooseneck overhang provides a lot of extra storage or living space.
- The extra size allows for more inclusions.
- Some find them much easier to handle.

Some fifth wheels are almost towable houses.

The major 'disadvantage' is that you need to hook it up to a utility vehicle. Whether this is a problem or not can be a bit subjective but for many the fifth wheels' advantages more than outweigh the disadvantages.

Tent Trailers, Fold Downs and Expandables

As the name implies these are trailer/tent hybrids. The trailer itself is a certain size in a rigid frame, but the usable living space is increased when you deploy tent-like extensions. They're basically a large tent in their own, easily transportable box, so they tend to suit the more outdoorsy types that are used to tents anyway.

Major advantages include:

- Their small size and light weight make them easy to manoeuvre.
- They can be towed even by a normal, family sedan car.
- They're inexpensive to buy, maintain and repair.

Disadvantages include:

- The interior space is limited, so storage is limited.

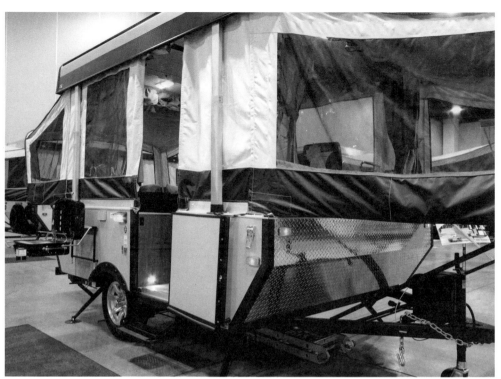

Tent trailers combine the portability and lightness of a tent, with the convenience of having a transportable base.

Some tent trailers are more rugged-looking than others.

Another option is this sort of arrangement, as long as you're happy to climb a ladder to get to bed, and climb down again if you have to heed a night-time 'call of nature'.

The Truck Bed camper might be a viable option if you don't want to spend *all* your money on your RV.

- They're more exposed to the weather, so they might not be suitable for extreme conditions.
- The hinges that make everything open up are a moving part subjected to stress, so you need to make sure that they're properly maintained so that they don't fail.

If you're planning to go to some of the more remote parts of Australia, like inland Western Australia and South Australia or Arnhem Land in the Northern Territory, a small tent trailer towed behind a high-clearance 4WD is actually your *only* option. Parks authorities won't allow any other sort of vehicle in places that are barely accessible by road.

Truck Bed Campers

Truck bed campers are becoming increasingly popular. Slide-in campers are not strictly towed so much as mounted and they're best imagined as mini fifth wheels, but without the wheels. Think of a metallic backpack that you slide in on the rear of a utility vehicle and that you can slide out and leave behind when you just want your truck on its own. If a tortoise could leave its shell behind now and again this is what this would be like and with few moving parts wear and tear is minimal. This is another rig with a lot of options, including expandable elements that can dramatically increase available size.

Truck bed campers are also very reasonably priced – you can start from as little as about $8000 with some of the more elaborate designs in the $30,000 range giving you many of the same amenities as towed trailers. Minimalist grey nomads might want to consider these as an excellent 'gateway' vehicle to introduce them to the life at a reasonable cost before committing to something bigger (or smaller). Of course, you can choose to be more elaborate but beyond a certain point you'll have to have a fixed, chassis-mounted truck bed camper, and those are pretty difficult to distinguish from a Class C. However, some companies will create a truck bed camper from your existing vehicle, so in this case they are effectively custom utility conversions.

Sport Utility RV Trailers and Toy Haulers

Imagine a box on wheels that has compartments for both living and sleeping spaces as well as spaces for sports vehicles such as snow mobiles or dirt bikes and that's basically what you have here. They're unlikely to be the RV of choice for grey nomads unless you're very active and creature comforts are way down on your list of priorities. They are, however, extremely customisable within their size limitations; and size is the major limit here since you're basically taking up a lot of room for the sports vehicles. Toy haulers are essentially live-in garages on wheels and this is important to note as your proximity to your vehicle might expose you to hazardous materials.

Due to the huge variety of trailers and their pluses and minuses, it really pays to do your research. Also note that trailers have to be registered, and different sizes and even wheel configurations incur different charges so this has to be factored into your costs.

Towing Vehicles

While there's no such thing as an 'ideal' towing vehicle, the general consensus for Australian conditions is that you'll need an all-terrain vehicle unless you plan to severely limit the number of places that you can go. The more range the better. About 450 kilometres (280 miles) is average and anything above 500 kilometres (310 miles) between refuels and you're doing very well.

The vehicle should have a lot of torque, or in the common vernacular, 'grunt' – the capacity to translate a lot of the engine's power into pulling strength, not necessarily speed. But torque isn't everything and it's crucial that the vehicle grips the road well, which often means that it's heavy enough to provide stability for the tow.

Handling is crucial. The vehicle should be highly manoeuvrable (small turning circles are nice if you can get them) because that gives you lots of options in difficult conditions. Considering the state of some of Australia's roads, you'll need excellent suspension too. And don't forget that not all towing vehicles handle towing downhill as well as they do towing uphill. Handling should be balanced against the need for stability, which often comes as a result of a long wheelbase, but that tends to impinge on handling, so you need to determine what's best for your needs.

The vehicle needs to be able to handle the *full* weight of the towable RV. The real test is when the RV is full of your stuff and you need to allow for what you can carry in the tower too. Note that towable RVs that weigh more than 4500 kilograms when full come with extra legal requirements such as needing to be fitted with air brakes.

Another consideration is if you want your tower to be a wagon or a utility vehicle, which is necessary if you have a fifth wheel assembly. And the vehicle should be fitted with a powerful front winch, which you might never need, but you'll certainly miss if you don't have it.

Once again this is a case of try before you buy and asking for different points of view from people who are more experienced than you. If you're buying everything from scratch, consider buying the tower around the needs of the vehicle that you'll be towing, rather than the other way around.

Whatever towing vehicle you finally decide to get, make sure it's powerful enough and versatile enough for your needs both present and future.

There are a number of useful articles on the different towing options on the FRC website:

www.frc.camp/towingpart1
www.frc.camp/towingpart2
www.frc.camp/towingpart3

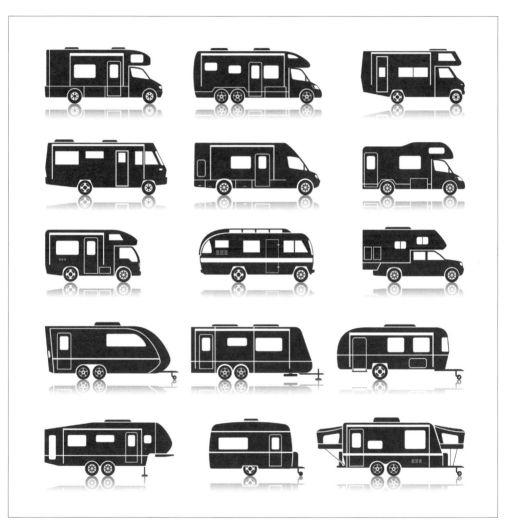

Different RV types at a glance: from top left to bottom right: 1,2, 3 Class C motorhomes; 4, 5 large Class B campervans; 6, 7 small Class C motorhomes; 8 older-style Class C; 9 truck bed camper; 10, 11, 12 caravans; 13 fifth wheel; 14 small caravan; 15 caravan with extensions.

Semi-Nomadism: The Tiny House

The tiny house movement is an international phenomenon that is only just starting out in Australia. The jury is still out on whether tiny houses are just a fad or whether they represent a major paradigm shift in the way that people are choosing to live.

There is no strict definition as what constitutes a 'tiny house', however, a general rule of thumb is a portable habitation of less than 37 square metres (400 square feet). This generally means that the footprint of a tiny house is about 2.6 x 14.3 metres (8.5 by about 47 feet). These measurements are defined by the upper limits of what is allowable on US roads while at the same time not needing a planning permit, but the situation is confusing as the law hasn't caught up with reality yet. The situation in Australia is even more ambiguous, with tiny houses occupying a weird niche between a trailer and a 'transportable building'.

You could fill a book with all the details about designing and living in a tiny home. There are a number of good books on tiny houses and there's an excellent YouTube channel dedicated to the subject, 'Living Big in a Tiny House'.

As far as the grey nomad is concerned, the tiny house is much less expensive to build and maintain than a conventional house and is also much less expensive than a mobile home or trailer, both to build and to maintain. The major downside is that a tiny house is much less transportable than a mobile home or trailer and is totally unsuitable for outback conditions or roughing it.

However, it might be the perfect solution for a 'semi-nomad' who likes their creature comforts. A semi-nomad would probably be moving seasonally and have very well-defined sites, reasonably close to civilisation, that they'd stay in for about three months at a time in areas where the local council has a relaxed attitude to alternative ways of living. If semi-nomadism is your style then the tiny house might be just the thing for you.

The portable tiny house is either a large caravan or a very small house, depending on your point of view and a viable option for the semi-nomad who likes their creature comforts.

Which RV is Right for You?

After an introduction to the various types of RV and all their pluses and minuses you might find the choices and options daunting. To help simplify your decision, here are the things you need to consider:

- How much money do you have? How much regular income will you be able to rely on? Remember, the purchase price of the rig is just part of the overall expense. You have to factor in total costs to your equation based on your guaranteed income.

- On average, how many people will be *regularly* sleeping in the rig? There's no point in lugging around extra capacity for the times the kids and grandkids come to visit if those visits are rare.

- How important are creature comforts to you? If you need a certain minimum standard of comfort then you're going to need to give yourself that or you're going to have to lower your expectations and adapt. Either way, there's no point in saving money and downsizing on luxuries, both big and small, if you're going to be miserable the whole time.

- How involved are you going to be with upkeep, maintenance and repair? If you're handy, that's great, but if you're going to outsource all maintenance then you have to factor in paying people to do it.

- Where are you going? If you're only going to travel within a limited area, always staying at favourite campsites then that's going to place one set of demands on your RV. If you're going to travel constantly all over Australia in all climates and conditions that's going to place an entirely different set of demands on your RV.

- Towable or non-towable? If you're going towable, then the selection of the tow vehicle becomes absolutely crucial (page 135).

- The devil is in the detail and RVs come with a lot of different options; you need to educate yourself about the various different options of every feature that's available to you (page 143).

Brands, Brands, Brands

The RV market is a specialist one. It's a tough gig to come up with a great RV that people love, and, as should be obvious by now, there is no such thing as the 'ideal' rig that will suit everyone.

The industry is dominated by a few well-established brands, but newer brands are emerging all the time with innovative ideas and approaches that give the establishment a run for its money. The world of RVs is a surprisingly big one with a huge range of pricing and configuration options. What constitutes value for money is up to you, but it pays to shop around.

A useful way to get educated about all your options is to watch a lot of YouTube videos. There are a number of YouTube channels that are dedicated to camping and the nomadic lifestyle but if you're specifically looking for RV design options then have a look at 'Mind's Eye Design'. They don't just cover camping but the producers evidently have a soft spot for recreational vehicles.

The list of RV brands, while not endless, seems endless; however, currently in Australia, the Caravan Industry Association (**www. caravanindustry.com.au**) is trying to battle the growing number of imports that are coming in that don't meet Australian standards.

Some brands that are popular in Australia vary tremendously in quality. Some are good value for what you get, just don't take them off road. Unfortunately, there are so many *unregulated* caravan manufacturers in Australia that it is starting to cause a problem. In the interest of keeping people informed as to what is going on, FRC publishes quite a few of the articles coming out of the Caravan Council of Australia (**www.caravancouncil.com.au**). Feel free to explore both these websites to keep abreast of industry news that might affect you as a consumer.

And feel free to go to a camp ground and speak to people there, see what rig they have, ask them why they made that particular choice, find out if there have been any extraordinary issues, especially about any modifications they might have made or any options they chose and how they feel about them now. This is as close as you'll get to an unbiased opinion.

Details, Details, Details and the Art of Customising or Even Converting a Vehicle

It's so important to select the right RV *for you*. Commercial RVs range from what you see is what you get to 'This is only an approximate idea of what you could have and there are all sorts of options and add-ons we can tempt you with beyond our base model'. This is where you'll need to really think about customisation. And, of course, in some cases, no matter how many vehicles you look at none of them seem right and you might be tempted to convert an existing one into something that's totally right for your needs.

Conversion is obviously not a job for the faint-hearted or under-skilled, but that hasn't stopped many people from just throwing themselves in at the deep end and coming up with a workable, self-created RV.

The thought processes and decision-making processes for customisation and conversion are quite similar, which is why we're going to introduce you to a checklist of points to consider whether you're choosing commercial or going your own way.

Whatever you decide to do, the end result has to be roadworthy. This is obviously not a problem with commercial customisation as manufacturing companies and dealers have to comply with the law. However, if you do it yourself, you're still going to have to comply with the law, so make sure that whatever you do is legal and results in a vehicle that can be legally registered, or you're going to be in for a lot of trouble and a lot of work could go to waste. Nevertheless, doing it yourself to roadworthy standards is well within the capacity of a lot of people. There are a huge number of stories out there. You can start with this one:

www.frc.camp/honky

Van? Truck? Bus? The size of the base vehicle will determine what is possible in terms of layout and how many features you can fit in. Converting a smaller vehicle isn't necessarily less work than a larger vehicle, because smaller vehicles require considerable design planning to maximise available space.

Common Challenges

Height, width and length of the vehicle have to be maintained within legal limits and there's not much wiggle-room here.

Weight: Mass is a hugely important consideration. How heavy will the vehicle be when everything you want is accounted for? Every extra gram will create extra stresses on the RV and add to fuel and

Custom conversion is always an option, and the VW Combi remains a perennial favourite.

maintenance costs. It's not just total weight you have to think about, but how weight is distributed in the RV. If one side or one end is considerably heavier than the other it creates all sorts of balance and handling problems. With bad distribution there are also uneven stresses and wear and tear on structural elements and moving parts. This is also a consideration even if you've bought your RV 'off the rack'. Weight/mass distribution is *always* important.

Security: What measures are available to prevent unwanted entry or theft? How does the vehicle lock? What anti-theft devices are available?

Safety: Consider fire alarms, extinguishers and other safety features. Smoke detectors have been mandatory in all new RVs in Australia since 2013 but older RVs might not have them. Carbon monoxide (CO) is colourless, odourless and can be deadly in a confined space and is usually the result of incomplete combustion of a gas stove. It can accumulate to deadly levels inside a cabin if it's not properly vented. You should have both smoke and CO detectors fitted in your RV. If the RV has LPG it would pay to have an LPG detector too in case of leaks.

Ventilation: Airflow is vital considering the above points and also considering that RV spaces are relatively small and confined. Dangerous gases can accumulate so quickly as a result of equipment use and even just normal human metabolism. It's not unknown for people to die from accumulation of the carbon dioxide that we naturally exhale. Ventilation is also a comfort issue as a way of regulating temperature and unpleasant odours.

Gas: The main use of gas for RVs is in cooking and sometimes for heating and water heating. Where will the gas be fitted and how are gas bottles stored? Is there an option for plugging in to mains gas?

Electricity: Solar, generator or both? Is there provision for external electricity? What surge protection do you have? Can you store power? If so, where are the batteries? How are the batteries charged?

Whether or not to take advantage of Australia's abundant sunlight as a source of energy is worth particular attention. Electricity is a clean option for heating and cooling, but it has to come from *somewhere*. If you don't go solar the electricity is going to have to come from either a campsite or be generated from petrol or diesel that you're burning. Considering that so much of Australia is hot and arid there might be many a day when you'll be inside your RV, sitting in air-conditioned comfort and blessing every second and every extra dollar you spent to go solar and use abundant, reliable, low-cost energy. This is a huge topic, worthy of a book in itself but at the very least consider this option.

Water: Where is water stored? Is water heating linked to space heating? How does the RV handle wastewater? Is grey water recyclable in the toilet? Is black water handled using a cassette system or a hose, or are both options available?

Lighting: What sort of bulbs are installed? How easy is it to get replacement bulbs? Is the RV equipped with outdoor lighting?

Heating and cooling: What's the heating and cooling power source and mechanism? How is temperature controlled or regulated within the spaces?

Bedding: How much do you need? Should it be permanent or modified from seating? Do you need a mixed-bedding strategy? Remember that non-permanent bedding has to be set up every night.

Showering and bathing: Does this happen indoors, outdoors or both? Is the shower space usable for any other function when it isn't a shower? How do you light an outdoor shower at night? How do you separate wet and dry spaces?

Toilet: RV toilets are increasingly becoming an item of major importance. Indoor or outdoor? If indoor is the toilet in the shower space (a wetbath) or separate? Can grey water from the shower be used in the toilet? Is a rinse wand available for 'stubborn areas'? What type of toilet: portable, conventional, water-free, composting, macerating, vacuum, other? Remember that many national parks won't let you in unless you take everything out with you too, including your blackwater, so blackwater holding might be a major consideration. Also, the vast majority of RV buyers nowadays prefer to have some sort of indoor toilet. An RV without one is at a major disadvantage in a resale. For an introduction to various toilet types go to '9 Kinds of RV Toilets: "Tour De Toilet"': **www.youtube.com/ watch?v=TFmcA0rWEFw**

SPECIAL TOILET NOTE: There are a number of water treatment options available for both black and grey water tanks. They allow you to control odour and break down bio matter. Other products help protect rubber seals and bio matter in breakdown seawater when freshwater is at a premium. *BioMagic* is an effective product and one of the only products that is permitted to be used in National Parks. HOWEVER, check with each state's National Park guidelines before emptying toilets in National Parks.

www.biomagic.com.au/concentrate-for-all-waste-tanks

Visit the FRC website for a 20 per cent discount on all BioMagic products.

Cleaning: How easy is it to keep the RV clean? Where do you store your cleaning products? How do you handle garbage and general waste?

Laundry: Is there room for a washing machine? Is washing and drying separate or do you have a combination unit? Where do you store dirty clothes?

Storage: Where do you put stuff when it's not in use? How do you separate different types of storage: food from clothing, dangerous chemicals and tools? How do you stop items from moving or breaking when in transit?

Battening down: When you have to shut everything down is this an easy process (as simple as pressing a button or shutting a door) or does it require forethought and planning?

Maintenance: How easy is basic maintenance, including mechanical work? Are all the parts of the RV relatively easy to access both inside and outside?

Communication: An increasingly important consideration as the more tech-savvy and tech-dependent generations get closer to grey nomadding age is whether or not the RV is equipped to handle mobile internet and the recharging of mobile phones, tablets, laptops or other technology.

Garaging: This is an often-overlooked factor. When not in use, is your RV properly protected or garaged? What provisions do you have to make to ensure that the RV is safe when not in use?

Accessorising: 'Accessory' is a wide-ranging term that includes everything from amenities to appliances to fit-out to interior design and finishes. It's easy to go crazy with accessories and every extra can add up. There's no easy answer to when you start overcapitalising, but if your RV is going to be your home it's important that you end up with something that suits *you*. Remember, that if you don't please yourselves (as much as you reasonably can) then the whole exercise of changing your life becomes worthless.

Security

Although it's possible for thieves to break into your home and steal stuff, it's almost unheard of that they steal the whole house. However, an RV is a vehicle. It is designed to move and be moved. In spite of Australia being one of the safest countries in the world , it is conceivable that if you don't secure your RV properly it could be vandalised or stolen. If your RV is stolen this effectively means that they've stolen your house, and, possibly, all of your worldly possessions. It's therefore really important that you take steps to make the theft of your RV as difficult as possible. You have one great advantage here though, an RV is difficult for thieves to offload and therefore RVs are not targeted nearly as often as cars or motorbikes, but that doesn't mean that thieves can't cause you considerable inconvenience, damage or heartache. So seriously consider security precautions no matter where you are. At the very least, consider the following:

- Install a new lock on your RV that's different from the manufacturer's one.
- Use chains and padlocks where appropriate.
- Install a security mesh door, if practicable.
- Install a GPS tracking device, well-hidden so that thieves won't be able to find it, or even suspect that it's there.
- Use hitch locks and wheel locks.
- Make sure that you're properly covered by insurance.
- Ask neighbours that you trust to keep an eye out.

Keeping It All Dry

As annoying as arid conditions are with ever-present dust that seems to get everywhere, it's moisture that is potentially much more problematic. The 'water where you don't need it' issue comes from three sources – external, internal and metabolic.

External water is rain and, more rarely, fog and mist. Rain is only a problem if there's a leak somewhere or if it just goes on for too long. Being stuck for days and days on end in a confined space will test even the strongest of relationships and particularly so if there are animals involved. Every time you go out for any reason you're going to get wet, and that might mean mud that will have to be cleaned up. Then there's all the damp clothes. Some of the larger RVs actually have wet rooms that allow for space where you can just get your wet self in order and hang your clothes up for drying but this is exceptional. For the most part you're going to have to find some way of having as easy a transition as possible during wet weather so that you're not bringing any more water into the RV than you absolutely have to.

Internal water comes from two main sources. If you have internal propane gas cooking then water will form as a normal by-product of propane combustion, increasing the amount of water vapour in the air. There's also the environmental water from cooking and, say, steam from showers. Usually this excess water leaves because of ventilation but if you're in cold conditions and you've got the windows, vents and doors shut all the time, the water has nowhere to go and builds up in the cabin.

One source of water that people tend to neglect is metabolic water. The average adult loses two litres of water a day, and not all of it goes down the toilet. Anything from half a litre to one litre per person leaves the body through perspiration and in the breath. But just because you can't see it, doesn't mean it isn't there, and in the closed confines of an RV in cold weather the water in the air condenses on the walls of the RV, like beads of moisture on a cold glass on a cold day. This cools the RV even more and you get a sort of reverse greenhouse effect. It's conceivable that you could get seriously ill as the moisture makes everything mouldy. Although we normally associate mould with warmth, there are plenty of moulds that like it cool, as anyone who has ever seen a neglected refrigerator can attest. So cold wet is just as bad as warm wet. In more acute extreme cold conditions then ice actually begins to form in the cabin and you'll find that you're effectively inside a refrigerator.

The cure to all this excess moisture is relatively simple. In warm humid conditions your best friend is a dehumidifier, but remember to close all your windows and vents first, otherwise your little humidifier is going to be trying to take all the water our of the rainforest you're in. In cold weather, you'll have to heat the cabin to at least 10 degrees Celsius and only then turn on a dehumidifier to suck all the moisture out. Dehumidifiers won't work until the temperature is at least 10 degrees. Whatever you do, you have to get the moisture out of the air, so heat *and* dehumidify!

Australia likes to sell itself in all the brochures as a warm to hot country, but this continent-sized island has plenty of room for eight climactic zones that vary through the year and if you plan to travel in the cold, you're going to have to plan for it.

Your Lifestyle, Your RV

After you've educated yourself and considered a number of options the choice of your RV comes down to questions of lifestyle. How do you live? How do you want to live?

If you're the outdoors type you might not need many creature comforts – just enough to ensure hygiene and safety, since your RV in such a case is essentially a portable bedroom, bathroom and kitchen. Your priority then becomes storage for outdoor equipment.

If you're somewhat more indoorsy either by choice or by necessity, you'll need to allow for more space within your RV. It would pay then to observe yourself as you go about your everyday settled life and ask yourself, 'How would I simplify this? How would I minimalise that?' You could also observe how you move within spaces, how you handle equipment, how much room your body takes up.

If you're honest with yourself, you might find that even though you might have lots of clothes, you tend to wear the same things. You don't need 101 outfits and if you choose your clothes and accessories carefully you can get a lot of variation from only a relatively few items. You also need to consider that your laundry facilities are going to be a bit more limited and you might have to be more careful about things like colour fastness.

Similarly, though your kitchen might be full of equipment you use the same frying pan over and over. Once again, carefully chosen equipment can be very versatile. For more on cooking and eating, see page 202.

And depending on your work then having a home office in your RV might be vitally important, or not important at all.

Look upon selecting or designing your RV as an opportunity to observe how you *really* live, not how you *think* you live, and then creating a personal portable living space that complements that life.

Big Recommendation: Try Before You Buy

No matter what type of RV you choose, we strongly recommend that you try it out before you commit to buying it. If you know the right people and have the right friends, you could borrow one for a bit. Or, you could rent. Although renting some rigs for a week or two might seem expensive, if it turns out you hate driving it or living in it then that will be money well spent on your education. If it turns out that you love that particular RV then that's money well spent too, because now you know exactly what you want.

New or Used?

The decision to buy a new or used RV isn't necessarily straightforward. New has the advantage of being covered by a warranty, but new vehicles also incur taxes that used vehicles don't have. On the other hand, a used vehicle might not need the warranty if it's been well looked after.

Strange as it might seem, new isn't always best because a lot of new vehicles haven't really been given the acid test of use and you might find that with a new vehicle there are a few teething issues to work out. Consider buying a used vehicle from a reputable dealer or other trusted source as you could be in for a bargain on a vehicle that has been road tested and where every little kink has been identified and worked out.

Do your usual due diligence when buying either new or used, especially used. If you end up with a lemon RV it's going to leave a really sour taste. Naturally, budgetary considerations come into play, and a good, reasonably comprehensive checklist or two:

www.frc.camp/checklist and www.frc.camp/predelivery

Financial Tips for RVs and the Realities of Depreciation

Like any other vehicle, finance is available for RVs if you don't want to lay out all the money in one go. This might be an advantage to you if you have a mobile business because interest payments on financing might be tax deductible (check with your accountant).

Fortunately, Australia has some of the strictest financial disclosure laws in the world. Financial advisors, or those selling you financial products, are obligated to disclose if they have a financial interest or receive some sort of remuneration from the lender. They are also obligated to disclose how much the total cost of financing will be if you only make minimal payments on a loan, and the cost of late payments and penalties, so there's no excuse not to know the real costs of the commitment you're making if you choose to go down the financing road for your rig.

One really important point to note is that, in the vast majority of cases, no matter how elaborate, expensive or well-equipped it is, *your rig is not an investment,* at least not a financial investment. A financial investment happens when you get more money back than what you originally spent. You could spend $300,000 on a house or an apartment (at least in some parts of the country) and be pretty confident that, well-maintained and even renovated, it will almost inevitably appreciate in value. This is not the case with a motorhome. A motorhome depreciates in value almost from the second that you sign on the dotted line. In fact, the depreciation rate on larger RVs (like Class As) and four-wheel drives is greater than for smaller RVs. For tax purposes the effective life of large RVs is only five years and for smaller RVs it's eight years. This might, or might not be to your advantage, depending on how you arrange your finances. However you cut it, it's unlikely that you'll get back what you paid for an RV, especially a motorhome, and it's almost unheard of that you'll actually make a profit on the resale. However, should you at some point want to stop nomadding you can still recoup at least some of your initial outlay.

The point about the depreciation of your RV is only to make it clear that purchasing an RV is not an investment in a financial sense. The change to nomadding might be incalculably and immeasurably valuable to you in a lifestyle sense. It might be worth every cent that you 'lose' in exchange for a richness of experience that you might never have had otherwise. It all depends on how you define wealth. What is a rich, full life worth to you?

And, having said that, there's no reason to believe that you can't be a nomad and get some financial profit out of it too, if you play your cards right. See pages 58 to 69.

[Source: www.depreciationrates.net.au/motorhomes]

Sunset on the Murray River at Renmark.

Stromatalites at Hamelin Pool in Western Australia.

A typical day in Coober Pedy.

Overspending on the Rig –
How to Unbalance the Budget

There's no doubt that some rigs are, by RV standards, palatial. The temptation that bigger is better is certainly there. When it comes to the potential comfort and style bigger usually is better, if you have some money to throw around then it's hard to resist that voice that says, 'Why not?'

In the course of researching this book there were quite a number of grey nomads and people who work in the camping support industries who were happy to share their stories. One particular type of story tended to stick out – the overcapitalisation story. Put simply, what happens is that a grey nomad couple gets all excited about selling their house and using the money to go all-out on a super-duper Class A motorhome. But what many couples failed to realise is that the motorhome is only the beginning of the expenses. They fail to consider running costs and other costs associated with nomadding, and in particular, how much these costs would impact on their disposable income, completely unbalancing their budgets. The result is that these couples end up in a big rig that's expensive to run, to the point that they are barely able to afford the normal expenses of living. They end up living in palaces, but like paupers. They have bitten off a lot more than they can chew. And they end up being laughing stocks because savvier nomads and more experienced campers can easily see the signs of people who have bought a white elephant. And it's a dangerous position to be in, because if you get into trouble that isn't covered by insurance, you can break the bank.

This is not an argument against Class As. They are easily the most comfortable way to nomad and would be the first choice of many people if they had the means. But that's the point. You have to be able to afford them. If you can't, you'll be buying into some heavy-duty financial stress that might leave you losing tens, if not hundreds of thousands of dollars. And that stress would defeat the whole purpose of the nomad way of life.

Don't become Mr and Ms overcapitalised, overextended and overwhelmed. Do your research, talk to people who are already doing this and find out the real costs before you commit.

ON THE ROAD

///

Grey Nomadding on the Road

The nomad lifestyle is, by definition, one of movement. The whole point of nomadding is to go to different locales to experience what they have to offer. This means dealing with roads in all sorts of conditions and being aware of how road conditions will affect your travel plans.

The Big Lap

The term 'big lap' refers to the circumnavigation, by road, of the Australian continent. This is generally done going along Highway 1, the M1, the interconnected highways that run the rim of the country, mostly, but not exclusively, along the coast.

The trip takes many people about a year, or longer. If you're starting in the south in summer then people usually travel counter-clockwise to take advantage of the prevailing winds – this means travelling west to east then north in the spring/summer months, and east to west then south in the autumn/winter months. Note however that the northern wet season that can seriously affect your travels hits north of the Tropic of Capricorn anytime from November to May, but generally peaks mid-December to April.

The M1 connects: Melbourne (with a side detour to Hobart), Sydney, Brisbane, Cairns, Darwin (with a major detour off the M1 to Alice Springs and Uluru if you're so inclined), Port Headland, Perth, Esperance, Adelaide, then back to Melbourne.

The M1 is sealed, so you don't need a four-wheel drive, but road conditions vary a lot – from multi-lane freeways to single-lane roads. If you want to take side journeys to some of the more rugged places that connect to the route, you'll need a vehicle capable of low gears and those in the know generally recommend a turbo-diesel engine for its efficiency and the fact that diesel is more readily available in remote areas than petrol.

If you plan a lot of off-the-beaten-track stuff, you're probably better off using a high clearance four-wheel drive and towing a smaller trailer than using a motorhome. This is one of those cases where you have to decide how mobile you want to be.

You'll need to be a bit cashed up if you plan to do things like frequently stay at campsites and don't want to skimp on eating in restaurants – to the tune of about $150 per day for a couple. It's always possible to do this for far less, but fuel is something that you won't be able to avoid spending on if you plan to travel the huge distances involved. Remember to budget for the occasional toll as well.

Road Conditions

There are over 900,000 kilometres of road in Australia, of which only about 350,000 are paved with the other over 560,000 unpaved, so road conditions and the skills and awareness to negotiate them play a major part in the nomadding experience.

Here are some things to factor into your decision-making processes when you're driving around.

Dust, Dust, Dust

If there's any problem besides unwanted moisture (page 148) that's a major issue in Australia, it's dust. Australia's arid environment and winds have had thousands of years to grind sand into a fine powder. Even some of the commercially built caravans and camper trailers will

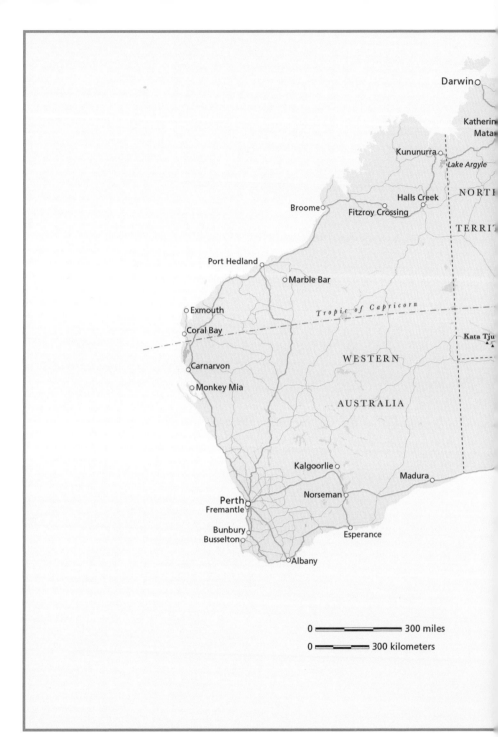

Darwin ○

Katherin
Mata

Kununurra ○
Lake Argyle

NORTH

Halls Creek ○

Broome ○   Fitzroy Crossing ○

TERRI

Port Hedland ○

○ Marble Bar

○ Exmouth

○ Coral Bay

Tropic of Capricorn

Kata Tju

WESTERN

○ Carnarvon

○ Monkey Mia

AUSTRALIA

Kalgoorlie ○

Madura ○

Perth ○
Fremantle ○

Norseman ○

Bunbury ○
Busselton ○

Esperance

○ Albany

0 ▬▬▬▬▬ 300 miles

0 ▬▬▬▬▬ 300 kilometers

Waters
oKarumba
oCairns
Tennant Creek
Mount Isa
Charters Towers o
oTownsville
oWinton
oBoulia
lice Springs
oRockhampton
QUEENSLAND
oBirdsville
Charleville o
Roma
o Oodnadatta
Lake Eyre
St George
Brisbane o
oCoober Pedy
SOUTH
Lightning Ridge o
AUSTRALIA
oBourke
Coffs Harbour o
Wilcannia
NEW
Broken Hill
Port Macquarie o
Port Augusta o
SOUTH
oDubbo
WALES
o Newcastle
in Bay
Adelaide
oHay
oSydney
Lincoln
Canberra
oWollongong
Victor Harbor o
A.C.T.
Albury
o Canberra
VICTORIA
Mt Kosciuszko
oBatemans Bay
Bendigo
oJindabyne
Ballarat o
Geelong o
oMelbourne
Timboon o
Apollo Bay o
Devonport o
oLaunceston
TASMANIA
oHobart
o Port Arthur

not be prepared for Australia's bull dust and it's especially prevalent in outback Queensland, the Northern Territory and Western Australia.

Bull dust is so fine, it will get through the very slightest of cracks in your rig and it will get into everything. After, say, a trip to Charleville in Queensland, which might involve a 60-kilometre side trip along a dirt road to a campsite, you could spend days cleaning the dust out.

It pays to thoroughly dustproof your rig. And once you've done a great job on your own, you can go into business dustproofing other people's rigs.

Weather and Natural Disasters

Something as simple as being alert to or actually paying attention to weather warnings can save you a lot of grief and hundreds, if not thousands, of dollars in repairs. Awnings blown off in strong winds are one of the most common occurrences for nomads and we hear from insurance companies that it's one of the more frequent claims.

You'll need to avoid certain areas if you know there is prolonged rain coming up. The FRC app has its own weather forecast capability built into the app. It shows a seven-day forecast at a glance at each and every campsite, which helps with your advanced planning. You can also set that alerts can be sent to your phone via the app to advise you of strong wind warnings in your area.

And even though natural disasters are nothing to wish for, they can also provide people with an opportunity to help where help is most needed:

www.frc.camp/helpaftercyclone

Left: The other side of dry, dusty Australia is wet, soggy Australia. Both have their charms and challenges.

Animals on the Road

We're usually talking kangaroos here, but we're not just talking about the odd kangaroo. It is conceivable that you could be in a situation where you could be wiped out by a whole mob of over a hundred kangaroos.

The other thing some nomads get a little overwhelmed with is the number of dead roos on the road. Sometimes you'll see a stretch of

tens of roos in a length of only 20 kilometres of road. Droughts tend to bring them to the side of the road and the trucks, and in some cases nomads in caravans, clean them up.

Other animals you'll see, both dead and alive, include emus by the dozens, camels galore, even eagles feasting on kangaroo carcasses in the middle of the road. Eagles rightly feel that you're in their territory, so they can take their time about flying away, so it's important to assess your speed when trying to avoid them.

And keep your eyes on the road. Running over a slow-moving tortoise makes a rather unpleasant 'crunch' sound that can spoil the whole day, especially if you're the sort of person who feels guilty about inadvertently killing wildlife.

Not one of the more pleasant pictures of the reality of Australian road travel, and certainly not one that you'll find in glossy tour brochures, but we're not here to lie to you and tell you that Australia is all fluffy bunnies, fairy floss and illustrations by May Gibbs. Roo roadkill is a fact of life that you'll have to get used to. Critical times to save both you and the roos from an unpleasant incident or potential mutual destruction are dawn and dusk, when kangaroos are at their most active.

Dealing with Road Trains

Road trains are either single units or convoys of large trucks usually transporting cargo. They're known as 'trains' because they involve some sort of articulation, with two and sometimes three trailers behind a main vehicle. Road trains are big and intimidating and, even though they don't mean to be, they are potentially dangerous. You'll find lots of road trains around the Nullarbor, making the cross-continental trip.

Your CB radio (page 191) will be your best friend here. Most truckies use channel 40, and if you make contact and state your intentions most will do their best to accommodate you. They will

Yep. Road trains are every bit as intimidating as they look.

tell you when it is safe to overtake, and if you are in front of them and you want *them* to overtake you, it is best to tell them first what your intentions are. Being overtaken by your first road train can be a little scary and overtaking one just as scary. You have to not only be aware of oncoming traffic but also any animals that may run out on the road. Some of the trains will let you know how many trailers they have, but some don't, so you don't really know if they have two or three trailers till you get right up beside them. The only drawback with having the CB on all the time is that some of the language from the truckies can be a bit colourful at times. Don't say we didn't warn you.

If you find yourself encountering a road train then a bit of discretion might be in order. Pull over to the side of the road, rest a bit. Let the road train pass. This is especially important during bad weather or if the road train picks up a lot of dust.

Parking and Rest Areas

There are 250 local councils spread throughout Australia and they vary hugely in friendliness, competence and frankly, intelligence levels. Some are a delight to deal with and some seem to have work cultures that go out of their way to make life difficult.

Some local councils actively encourage campers and nomads, others couldn't give a toss, so gathering information on parking and rest areas that are RV-friendly throughout the country is an ongoing challenge that FRC is nevertheless bravely attempting.

In the meantime, your next best friend for finding RV-friendly parking and rest areas is through local tourist information centres (TICs). You'll find contact details for TICs in the FRC Directory.

1. Login.
2. Go to the directory.
3. Select the state of your choice.
4. Select the category 'Tourist Information Centres' and then the map on your screen will show TICs with map markers at each location.

Rest Areas Versus Free Camps

As much as we all acknowledge the need for drivers to be well rested, there is, nevertheless, a war out there when it comes to staying overnight in rest areas. Most rest areas will be clear as to whether or not caravans can stay in them or not. There are some however that are *purely* designated for heavy vehicles. This is so that truckies can sleep.

Truckies can get very upset if a caravan pulls over in one of their areas. There are some instances where there are so many caravans using up designated truck space that there's no room left for them. This makes life for them impossible, because it is mandatory for truckies to rest as part of their work conditions. In some cases, they have been known to block the recalcitrant caravans in and not let them out and the odd fist-fight has occurred. There are currently movements out there to crack down on caravans abusing the rights of truckies. FRC and others have done their best to combat abuses where possible and to clearly distinguish what is a rest area versus what is a free camp and to further distinguish caravan rest areas as opposed to truck stop rest areas.

Roadside Assistance

Australia, in case you hadn't noticed, is a big place, and if you and your vehicle get in trouble it might be very difficult to get help unless you get insurance for roadside assistance and, if necessary, towing. Fortunately, Australia has some of the best motoring organisations in the world and no matter which state you're based in there's an organisation ready to help you out.

The fees are extremely modest, considering the coverage and benefits that you get. To give you an idea, even the Premium Plus Coverage (recommended for grey nomads) offered by the New South Wales and Australian Capital Territory-based NRMA, only costs around $60 for a one-off joining fee, plus around $30 per month – less if you pay a whole year in advance.

Even if you're travelling around, it's good to have some place to pick up your mail, so where you have a post box is usually going to be your 'address' even if you are a 'person of no fixed abode'.

As a result, people tend to join the association in the state or territory where they either spend the most time, pick up their mail, or where they actually have a fixed residence that they haven't given up in order to go nomadding.

Please note: the NRMA is a *national* association, so even though they're based in New South Wales they don't care where you live and will take members from anywhere. Their Premium Plus coverage has you covered no matter where in Australia you are when you call them. Other motor associations might have limitations on whom they allow to join, so it's best to check with them first.

Because of reciprocal arrangements between all the motoring associations, all roadside assistance in Australia is covered by one phone number: **13 11 11** that will direct you to the relevant, state-based motor association no matter who you're with, but the cover and benefits that you get will depend on which organisation you've actually joined.

Since everyone's circumstance and needs are different it's best to contact the association you're interested in and describe your situation exactly. They can then advise which membership plan would be best for you.

For further information:

New South Wales and Australian Capital Territory: National Roads and Motorists Association (NRMA); Phone: 13 11 22; website:

www.mynrma.com.au

Northern Territory: Automobile Association of the Northern Territory (AANT); Phone: 08 8925 5901; website:

www.aant.com.au

Queensland: Royal Automobile Club of Queensland (RACQ); Phone: 13 19 05; website:

www.racq.com.au

South Australia: Royal Automobile Association of South Australia (RAASA); Phone: 08 8202 4600; website:

www.raa.com.au

Tasmania: Royal Automobile Club of Tasmania (RACT); Phone: 13 27 22; website:

www.ract.com.au

Victoria: Royal Automobile Club of Victoria (RACV); Phone: 13 72 28; website:

www.racv.com.au

Western Australia: Royal Automobile Club of Western Australia (RAC); Phone: 13 17 03; website:

www.rac.com.au

Note that membership plans don't just offer roadside service. Many provide fuel and accommodation coverage, personal transportation costs, discounts at a number of different retailers and venues and even driver training.

Even the best membership plan won't necessarily cover *all* emergency contingencies. In some cases, an association will provide services outside of your plan for an additional fee. In other cases, you might have to find other, independent operators to cover additional services. This is especially true if you have a big vehicle that weighs more than 10 tonnes and requires heavy haulage to get you out of trouble.

Getting Out of Trouble – A Traveller's Tale

There are a million ways to get into trouble, and a million ways to get out of trouble. In the following story Rob Catania shares with us how even when things look bad, angels from the most unlikely places can come to the rescue and lead you to experiences you otherwise wouldn't have had.

We were in no hurry and on our way west to Johanna Beach, between Princetown and Cape Otway in Victoria. However, on the way there things were not right with the bus. It was revving excessively and losing power. The big hills didn't help and about 5 kilometres out of Apollo Bay something smelt like it was burning. We rolled down the hill into town and I headed straight for the local mechanic. When they heard it was a bus, they were very reluctant to come out and help us. But when I described what had happened, he said it was probably my clutch. That made sense.

I got on the phone to Bob and explained it all to him. He said the same thing. Probably the clutch. He suggested we not drive it if that was the case. We made a few calls, and there were no heavy vehicle repairers in Apollo Bay. The closest were either at Colac or Warrnambool, which is where we were heading to next. Then we had the added problem of getting it there. Everyone suggested not driving it, so the only option was to tow it. Being a Friday afternoon however, no one wanted to know us.

We ended up deciding to stay the weekend at Apollo Bay and wait till Monday morning to try and fix the problem. Feeling somewhat frustrated at the lack of help, Michelle went off to suss out the three caravan parks in town. The first one she came to was the showground caravan park. When she got there she was told there was only one spot left. She went to suss it out, and, lo and behold, there was a bus parked right next to the vacant spot. Under the bus she spotted two legs jutting out.

She of course got talking to the guy and told him of our troubles. He was very generous and offered to have a look at it for us. He was not a licensed mechanic, but he knew all about motors, as he worked on his own. Got to love the bush mechanics; they often know more than real mechanics. In this case he did. Anyway, this guy was going to drive out and see us, but she told him we had already booked in.

We struggled over to the site; it was only about 3 kilometres from where we stopped, but it was a slow trip with the clutch slipping the whole way. We virtually limped into the site. Then, within half an hour of stopping, Peter, the guy Michelle had found, had it fixed. It turned out it needed an adjustment and the clutch plate was slipping. This is what was causing the burning smell. Trouble was, we still had no idea of how much real damage was done. So, while we could at least now drive it, we still had to get the clutch looked at.

We were very grateful for Peter and to his wife Ryll. Earlier that day we had bought a kilo of prawns, and as they would not take any payment for the work he did to the bus, we invited them over to share dinner with us. There were really nice folk from Grafton and they even offered for us to join them on the rest of their trip, just in case we ran into further problems. We would have taken them up on the offer except we wanted to go slower and stop at Warrnambool.

We ended up staying at Apollo Bay for the rest of the weekend. And we were lucky enough to be there for the Annual Show.

Exploring the Cities

Your rig is ideally suited to travelling Australia's various highways, wilds and back-of-beyonds, and as your home. Depending on its size, it might not be all that convenient as an urban run-around. When hanging out in the capital cities, consider parking your rig somewhere where it's legal to do so and won't inconvenience anyone, and explore the city on public transport, using that city's transport passes to pay, and the appropriate app to navigate and plan your trips.

Adelaide: Metrocard; website:

www.adelaidemetro.com.au/Tickets-fares/metroCARD
www.adelaidemetro.com.au/Timetables-Maps/Mobile-apps

Brisbane: TRANSLink *go* card; website:

www.translink.com.au/tickets-and-fares/go-card
www.translink.com.au/plan-your-journey/mytranslink

Canberra: MyWay; website:

www.transport.act.gov.au/tickets-and-myway/get-myway
www.transport.act.gov.au/contact-us/apps

Darwin: Tap and Ride Card; website:
**www.nt.gov.au/driving/public-transport-cycling/public-buses/
fares/tap-and-ride-card
www.nt.gov.au/driving/public-transport-cycling/public-buses/
bus-tracker-app**
Hobart: Greencard; website:
**www.metrotas.com.au/fares/greencard
www.metrotas.com.au/communication/apps**
Melbourne: myki; website:
**www.ptv.vic.gov.au/tickets/myki
www.ptv.vic.gov.au/footer/about-ptv/digital-tools-and-updates/
mobile-apps**
Perth: SmartRider; website:
**www.transperth.wa.gov.au/SmartRider/Types-of-SmartRider
www.transperth.wa.gov.au/journey-planner/mobile-services/
official-transperth-app**
Sydney: Opal Card; website:
www.opal.com.au; www.transportnsw.info/plan

Adelaide

Brisbane

Darwin

Canberra

Hobart

Melbourne

Sydney

Perth

Saving on Fuel Costs and Estimating Fuel Costs

There are a number of ways that you can save money on fuel either by using less fuel, paying less for it, or getting other benefits when buying fuel.

Paying Less – the Price Cycle

As any experienced motorist knows, some days are better than others for buying fuel. But price optimisation for the consumer involves understanding that petrol prices move up and down according to regular cycles and these cycles vary from place to place. A useful and regularly updated tool for getting the best petrol deal is the Australian Competition and Consumer Commission's guide to petrol price cycles:

**www.accc.gov.au/consumers/petrol-diesel-lpg/
petrol-price-cycles**

And we've said it before, we'll say it again: the more weight you're handling the higher the fuel bill and the wear and tear on all the systems combined.

A fuel consumption of a combined gross mass of 20 litres per hundred kilometres (14 miles to the gallon) is pretty standard. The 900-kilometre trip from Sydney to Melbourne will necessitate 180 litres. At the top end of fuel prices at $1.65 per litre this means that the trip would cost $297 in fuel alone. At the bottom end at $1.25 per litre the trip would cost $225. That's a $70 difference, all hinging on where and when you buy. The expense is even greater in the outback, where you can pay up to $2.50 per litre or more.

Bear in mind that if you wait until the tank is near empty, you're at the mercy of whatever the price is. Although it's slightly more time consuming, if you make it a habit to top up when the fuel price is lowest, you're going to save money.

Petrol-tracking apps are now available that can clue you in to price alerts based on your postcode.

Consider Fuel Map Australia or MotorMouth:
www.motormouth.com.au

Another fuel-saving tip is to go easy on the accelerator. By easing into acceleration and deceleration you can save up to 20 per cent on your fuel consumption because you're not wasting fuel going full throttle. Remember that driving long distances, especially with a vehicle in tow, is an art worth your learning.

Rewards cards, like Woolworths Everyday Rewards or Coles flybuys have built-in petrol discounts if you pay with those cards too.

Mental Health Tip

It's easy to get obsessive over fuel costs and it's a favourite subject among certain nomadders, who get hung up on avoiding spending a few extra dollars here and there on fuel. However, things need to be put into perspective. The whole point of nomadding is to see the country. If obsessing over fuel costs is going to seriously impinge on your enjoyment then wait until you've saved up and budget accordingly. There's only so much you can do about the cost of fuel so just be prepared to pay the price to enjoy yourself.

Vital On-the-Road Tips

- Always work out the road conditions before you go. This information is relatively easy to come by through regular reports on commercial radio or if you learn how to use a CB radio (page 191) and politely extract information from other travellers.
- If you're travelling in pairs you cannot afford to delegate all the mechanical knowledge or emergency procedures knowledge to just one person. What if that person gets sick or is otherwise incapacitated? It is therefore crucially important that all members of a travelling team have at least some basic mechanical aptitude and can people out of trouble in an extreme situation, or, at the very least, keep things together until professional help arrives.
- Playing 'I Spy with My Little Eye' gets old really fast so think about things that you can do to keep yourselves entertained on those long drives. You might decide to learn a foreign language. You might listen to audio books. You might decide to listen to all that music you've been meaning to listen to for years. Now's your chance.
- Plan, plan, plan. Although this advice will fall on deaf ears to Mr and Ms Spontaneity, it's common sense to have an idea of where you want to go and when so that you're fully prepared for any reasonable eventualities, and some not-so-reasonable ones too.
- Don't forget to rest. There's a reason that the Australian government spent millions on the STOP – REVIVE – SURVIVE campaign. Driver fatigue is a major cause of

accidents but tired people still often ignore the signs of fatigue because they need to get somewhere. But, as the saying goes, it's better to be late than to be dead on time. Pull over and take a nap. If the police knock on your door and ask what you're doing just tell them that you're exhausted and you need to rest. They'll be very understanding and might even escort you to a better place to rest. And for more on the etiquette of rest areas see page 169.

- Consider using the timer on your smart phone to set alarms for every two hours. This will be your signal to stop for a few minutes, get out of your vehicle and walk around a bit, do some stretching. Even a five-minute break will do wonders for you.

This sturdy looking vehicle is what we mean when we say 'high-clearance 4WD'. The road beneath it, if you can even call it a road, is the reason why you need a vehicle like this one and the heartland of Australia is full of roads that look like this or worse.

Strictly speaking, for your vehicle to qualify, you need to have at least about 20.5 cm (8 inches) from the lowest point on the vehicle body to the ground, but you'd be hard-pressed to find any government or parks authority that would commit itself to that definition.

If you see a sign saying 'High-Clearance 4WD Only' then translate that as meaning 'Don't go here unless you have a vehicle that can handle it. You have been warned.'

Feel free to google '4WD Australia' or similar.

Staying Practical – Your Minimum Equipment

Considering that you have to think minimally anyway to save on weight, space, fuel and wear and tear on your rig and so that you don't have to spend too much of your life maintaining and keeping track of *stuff*, what's the minimum amount of stuff you need to take with you so that you're at least minimally safe, secure and presentable?

Personal items:

- First aid kit.
- Fire extinguisher.
- Minimal cooking equipment.
- Emergency survival rations.
- Water. Always, always, always carry extra, potable drinking water.
- Water purification tablets for emergencies at the very least, or, better, a water filtration system of some sort installed in your RV.
- Minimal clothing, with an extra emergency set for when you need to change in a hurry but can't wait to launder. Include protective clothing for any extreme conditions that you're likely to encounter.
- A really good pair of boots. You'll be wearing them a lot. Think about gel insoles too.
- A night light – the type you strap to your head or hat when

you need to go hunting about for something in the dark.

- Face netting to keep you sane from attacks by midges and sand-flies.

Aside from the minimum equipment you need for your personal items, there's a bare minimum you'll need for your **vehicular requirements:**

- Wheel replacement materials – jack, jacking plate, wheel replacement tools, spare tyre, tyre repair kit, air pump.
- Engine consumables – brake fluid, coolant, engine oil, spare fuel, jumper leads. Also, spare fan belts, radiator hoses and the necessary tools to replace them, since these are the most common things that fail but that don't need a mechanic to deal with them.
- Emergency repair kit including cable ties, fencing wire and gaffer tape.

We strongly recommend that you do some sort of **basic mechanical course and/or four-wheel drive course** specifically designed for bush and outback conditions, such as those conducted by:

- **www.australian4wd.com.au**; phone 07 3264 1877
- Getabout Training Services; **www.getabout.edu.au**; phone 1300 660 320
- If you happen to have a Toyota Land Cruiser, join the Toyota Land Cruiser Club of Australia and do the courses that are mandatory for their members; **www.tlcc.com.au**; phone 0408 736 472. Even if you don't have a Toyota, find out if there's a club that covers your particular make of RV. It's worth checking around to see what's available in your home state near you.

Vehicular get-out-of-trouble gear. We have it on good authority that getting bogged is almost inevitable at some stage and at the very least you'll need the following equipment:

- A long-handled shovel.
- Some sort of ramp arrangement, like a pair of Maxx Trax or a Bog Out **www.frc.camp/bogout.**
- An air compressor and a pressure gauge of good quality. One tried and tested method of getting out of being bogged down is to lower your tire pressure to around 20 psi (138 kPa). We recommend practising with this gear a few times in non-critical conditions so that you're experienced with getting out of trouble before you ever have to deal with this sort of situation in real life.

A snatch strap. A snatch strap is a length of elastic nylon webbing that effectively acts like a rubber band on steroids and helps another vehicle pull yours out of trouble. For a full description go here: **www.carsguide.com.au/adventure/how-to/how-to-use-a-snatch-strap-69116.** Do not underestimate the value of a snatch strap to help you get out of trouble. Read the story on page 187.

Emergency equipment. Satellite phone and satellite navigation if you plan to go way off the beaten track. Use only for emergencies as the cost is around $1 a minute, but what's that if it saves your life? The four satellite networks that cover Australia are:

- Globalstar: **www.globalstar.com**
- Inmarsat: **www.inmarsat.com**
- Iridium: **www.iridium.com** connected through Telstra.
- Thuraya: **www.thuray.com** connected through Optus.

One way of connecting is through the Thuraya Sat Safety bundle. It costs around $1000 and includes the phone (with a sat nav), charger and adaptor plugs in a waterproof case. Subscription costs $15 per month and calls are free to receive. Reception available throughout Australia and to over 160 other countries too. Contact Sat Phone Sales on 1300 135 457 or visit **www.satphonesales.com.au**

Note that satellite phone equipment is network specific so you can't use an Inmarsat phone on the Iridium network. Each network has its pros and cons and we recommend that you do your homework specific to your needs. If you're in luck, you might get a good deal on a prepay or post-pay deal.

Also consider flares and other signalling equipment.

A Snatch Strap Survival Story

In the following traveller's tale, Rob shows us how snatch straps can succeed when all else fails.

In Kununurra, the entrance to the Kimberleys, it was a long way across the top of the Great Sandy Desert, so we decided to have the bus checked out before we left. It was sort of OK, with the mechanic pinpointing what he described was a 'possible' noise in our gearbox, but he was of the opinion we would make it to Perth.

Our first stop was the Bungle Bungles, which were incredible. They looked like massive beehives, layered with black and red bands. It was the roughest road we had been on to get there, but a whole lot of fun.

We left the Bungle Bungles preparing for the long trip across to Derby. It is about 400 kilometres across passing through the towns of Halls Creek and Fitzroy Crossing. Then, something happened that drastically changed the course of the next few days. All of a sudden, I hear this little voice in my head, and next thing I know I am having a full-on conversation with myself. It had to be the heat. I was actually contemplating letting Michelle drive Honky. Before I could think about it logically, I spluttered it out loud, 'Would you like to drive for a while, Shell?

'OK,' she replied, the lack of hesitation scaring me.

The kids got all excited because Mummy was going to drive. Daddy was a bit nervous, but it was all good. We drove on for a while, Michelle gaining confidence the whole time. I was quietly proud of her. Then it was time to change back. I gave instructions on how to down gear. Sixth to fifth went OK. Fifth to fourth. Houston, we have a problem.

The gears won't shift. The clutch won't come out. Jammed solid. Panic.

Pull over. *Shit.*

Not really much room to pull over here. What to do? We slow enough to change seats, but it isn't much better for me. Gears and clutch are still stuck, and we are slowing. There is a slight incline on the side of the road and it levels out a bit, we have barely enough speed to get off the side of the road, coming to rest about 30 centimetres from the edge. We get onto the towing service from Derby. We explain the situation. Big bus, 13.5 tons. He asks for the clearances, front and back.

'I have a tilt tray that will do that,' he tells me.

'What about a flat tow?' I ask.

'Nah, the tilt tray will do it. $1200.'

Wow. Let me think about it: my wife and kids, 160 kilometres from town, surrounded by desert, 30 centimetres from the edge of the highway, the whole bus shaking from the wind as each road train roars past.

Ah, OK. Come and get us.

For two long hours we waited on the side of the road. Finally, just before dark, the tow truck turns up. He was pretty confident he would get us on, I was thinking otherwise. His tilt tray did just that, it tilted, steeper than Mt Kosciuszko. He started off by pulling us away from the edge of the road onto the level bit, then he tried to winch us on, successfully twisting the two 12 millimetre steel towing lugs and squashing our exhaust, moving us a total of about 1metre. There was no way known Honky was getting on that tray. It was like watching Beethoven, the giant Saint Bernard, refusing to budge on a leash.

So, there we stayed. The plan was to try again in the morning, but how exactly we weren't sure. It was a long night, a bit noisy with the trucks and dingoes howling, and did I mention we were only about 400 kilometres from Wolfe Creek? What a great night to watch the movie.

The following morning the tow truck owner rings, says he has a truck nearby and the driver will flat tow us in. They show up, this time in a semitrailer, with a large flat tray, and on the back of it, a large 6-tonne refrigerated truck, which has also broken down. He backs up in front of me and connects two oversize elastic bands to the front of Honky.

Being curious, I ask him what the snatch straps are rated at.

'About two and half tonne each,' he tells me.

I am not confident in the maths, but out here, my choices are limited. So here I am, nervously sitting in Honky, the plan being that I have the motor running so I have power steering and breaks. I am now to follow behind this semi, 7 metres away from the rear of the refrigerated truck. God, I felt so safe.

'We will go slow,' he tells me. Lucky by this time, I have sent Michelle well ahead with the kids in the Suzuki.

And slow we went, I watched with cheeks clenched tightly as those straps stretched to their fullest extent, anticipating that at any moment one would snap and come hurtling back through the windscreen, smashing it, along with my face. As they tightened, I could hear and feel the chassis of Honky screaming in pain. But we started to move. The whole 150-kilometre trip was done at 50 kilometres per hour. My task, to keep the straps tight, feather the breaks, and steer. If he stopped suddenly, I was in the cool room; if I stopped suddenly, I would cop a rubber band in my face. And to think I was *paying* for this.

We spent that night in the Derby Bus Depot, surrounded by buses. At least Honky was in good company. Then the following morning we get the good news. It's not the gear box. It's the clutch. Yes, the brand-new clutch we had fitted at

Warrnambool, 5000 kilometres ago, has shat itself. Not sure how, but that didn't really matter.

By Wednesday we got the news that Honky had been fixed and we could go and collect him.

Meet your new best friend – a snatch strap (right) with assorted paraphernalia. You'll deeply regret not getting one or learning how to use it.

Hamming It Up on the Radio

In Australia isolation is frequently lethal, so it pays to keep in touch. One relatively cheap way it to take advantage of citizen band radio, a two-way service that's short-range, but cheap, super-reliable and an excellent way of getting information on the ever-moving grapevine of drivers along Australia's highways. Users do not require a special licence to operate CB radios.

CB radio operates on two band ranges:
- High Frequency (HF) at 26.965 to 27.405 MHz
- Ultra-High Frequency (UHF) at 476.4125 to 477.4125 MHz

There are special call bands if you want to contact other travellers, after which you negotiate switching to another channel to continue the conversation:
- HF Channel 11 (AM – 27.085 MHz)
- HF Channel 16 (SSB – 27.155 MHz)
- UHF Channel 11 (476.675 MHz)

If you're clever you can transmit data through these dedicated, data-specific UHF channels:
- UHF Channel 22 (476.950 MHz)
- UHF Channel 23 (476.975 MHz)

And there are three emergency channels:
- HF Channel 9 (27.065 MHz)
- UHF Channel 5 (476.525 MHz)
- UHF Channel 35 (477.275 MHz)

For further information go to:
www.acma.gov.au/Citizen/TV-Radio/Radio/Marine-and-Amateur-Radio/citizen-band-radio-service-cbrs-fact-sheet

For those who are really keen go to The Wireless Institute of Australia:
www.wia.org.au/licenses/foundation/about

How a Short Range UHF Radio or Walkie-Talkie Can Save Your Relationship

Here's a story from Rob that illustrates one of the finer points of having a towing rig.

One of the greatest pieces of advice we were given when we started was to get a UHF radio. It's saved our marriage on more than one occasion. One of the funniest things you'll see is the daily ritual of one partner trying to help the other reverse a caravan. In fact, it's common entertainment to stop and watch when someone arrives at a campsite. The directions are all over the shop. One usually stands where the other can't see them. One yells out obscure messages, randomly, which of course the other cannot hear, because the one doing the directing is miles away behind the caravan.

Alternatively, you can just get yourself a UHF radio and guide the whole process without a fuss.

CB radios come in all shapes and sizes and having one is a very good idea whether you're on or off beaten tracks.

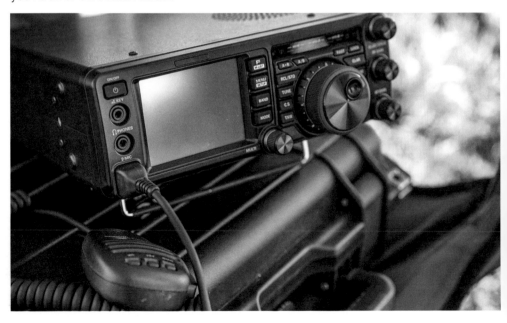

Navigating Through Cyberspace

Knowledge is power and if you have access to knowledge you have more choices and can make better decisions. One way of getting that knowledge is through those marvels of modern technology – the internet, mobile devices and their apps.

Let's face it. There are tech-savvy people and there are people who aren't. But whichever category you belong to, there are a whole bunch of online, internet-accessible tools available to the 21st century nomad that would have been the envy of travellers in past centuries and that can provide you with the knowledge you need to help you explore your options, plan your trips but also make informed choices.

At the very least, these tools can spare you some inconvenience. At the very best, they can save your life, or the life of someone you love.

The online tools are broadly websites and apps. Let's start with apps.

What Is an App?

For those of you who don't know, the word 'app' is short for 'application'. An app is a specialised program or piece of computer software with a specific *application*. It's basically a one-trick-pony program, but depending on your need, that pony's trick can be very, very valuable to you. Here are some of the tricks those ponies can do for a grey nomad.

They can:

- help you find places to stay and what facilities are available
- point out places to visit
- tell you where you can take your pooch, and where you can't
- suggest places to eat
- predict what the weather is going to be like
- show you where you are, how to get to where you're going, inform you of any traffic problems, tell you how long it's going to take, tell you how much fuel you'll need, tell you where to get it and even how much it's going to cost.

There are three types of app, and all of them work in slightly different ways, which might or might not affect the way you can access and use them. The important point here is that some apps work *only* when they're connected to the internet (when they're online), some don't have to be connected to the internet (they work offline) and some can work in both ways (both online and offline).

Desktop Apps

These work from your computer or laptop. Most people just call these apps software. They're usually the most robust form of an app and are often fully functional versions of a computer program. These are the apps you use when you have access to a home computer or a laptop, so you'll usually be at some sort of 'home base' when you use these apps and you generally use them with a keyboard or mouse. You will usually need to be connected to the internet to buy them and download them, but you don't have to be connected to the internet to use them, since, once downloaded, the app 'lives' inside your computer. However, apps, like all computer programs, need to be updated, so an internet connection is necessary when the app needs an update, and when you might want to use it to connect to other people.

Mobile Apps

As you might expect, mobile apps work from a mobile device – your smart phone or tablet. They are usually a stripped-down version of a full app, designed to give you just the most essential functions, or they are programs that are specifically designed only for use on mobile devices. These are apps designed for use with your finger on a touch screen and when you need a keyboard, a virtual one pops up for one- or two-finger typing. You don't need a mouse because your fingers, working directly on the touch screen, are your mouse. Like desktop apps (software), mobile apps don't necessarily require that you're connected to the internet after the initial download. However, because they are mobile-specific programs, connection to the internet is necessary if the app is designed to give you real-time, up-to-the-minute information.

Mobile device apps also generally come in two 'flavours' or platforms – Android and Mac, depending on whether your smartphone or tablet is based on the PC model, or if it's an Apple iPhone or iPad. Each type of device has its fans and the way that you use them is different. If you have an Android phone then your friend with the iPhone might not be of much help if you get into trouble. Some people can only use one type, while others are 'bi-digital'. It would probably be useful to understand at least a little of the other platform since you never know when you might need to use one system or the other.

Web-based Apps

These can be used either on your desktop or laptop, or on your mobile devices. In order to work you have to be connected to the internet, usually through your web browser, because the app doesn't 'live' in your device but exists in the mysterious world of cyberspace. With web-based apps, your computer or smartphone is simply a tool for talking to the app, so web-based apps don't need to be downloaded and you can use them directly through your browser. If you're in the middle of nowhere with no internet connection, a web-based app isn't going to be of much use to you, no matter how useful it might be when you do have an internet connection. Web-based apps are on their way out because of their limitations and because mobile devices are now powerful enough and roomy enough on the inside so that a lot of apps can 'live' inside them. That said, the number of apps that can live in your mobile phone or tablet depends on the one you have. If you're getting a new phone or tablet, it might be worth spending a few extra bucks for one with more memory, so that you can have plenty of room for apps that you might acquire.

A Note About the FRC App

The FRC app works in exactly the same way whether you have an Android or iOS device and it is designed to work both online (connected to the internet) and offline (not connected). This is a great advantage, as coverage around Australia is terrible, despite what Telstra and the federal government will tell you. The FRC app loads all current information about campsites directly to your phone or tablet and the information stays in your device. This way, you can still check out campsites and even navigate to them when you are offline. Of course, no updates will be included until you're back in range of an internet connection, at which time the app will automatically update.

Where to Get Apps

Generally speaking you get apps from specialist websites on the internet. These are either general app store sites or sites from the web developer themselves. General store sites include:

- Amazon's Appstore: **www.amazon.com.au** click on 'Apps & Games' in the search window
- Windows Store: **www.microsoft.com/en-au/windows/windows-10-apps**
- Apple App Store: **www.apple.com/au/ios/app-store**

In the world of apps, you don't always get what you pay for. Some really useful apps are free, while some pricey ones are only useful if you have very specific needs. We can only provide a general, introductory guide to the world of apps, and we strongly recommend that you read at least a few reviews of apps that you're considering. Remember that your smartphone can only take so much, so a few, well-chosen apps are better than a slew of ones that you'll only use rarely, if at all. Be particularly attentive to apps that are 'free' but require in-app purchases. The free version of an app usually has very limited functionality and is there so that you can try before you buy. To unlock the full potential and usefulness of an app you'll usually have to buy the full version. Fortunately, most mobile apps are very reasonably priced; although some of the more expensive apps are worth every penny, especially if you can get them on sale.

Another thing to watch out for is apps that are only available on subscription, where your right to use the app has to be renewed every year. This can work really well for you when you only need an app for a specific, short-term project. If you're a committed nomad, you might want to consider apps with a one-off payment or a lifetime membership, if one is available. Some of the best apps, however, are only available as renewable subscriptions, because developers have to cover the cost of updates and, in some cases, an out-of-date app can be worse than useless.

How to Use Apps

Like all things in the world of computers, using an app can be as simple or as complicated as you want it to be. Some people get by only using the most basic features of an app while others are able to take full advantage of the app's functions.

Success with an app is all about how easy it is to use, what it can and can't do, and how much you're willing to learn. Clarity is important here. Enjoy the fact that there is an app that has something to offer you and don't complain if your app doesn't do something that it wasn't designed to do. That's like complaining that a hammer doesn't do a good job of being a screwdriver.

As we emphasise time and time again, when you're out in the big, wide world in situations where the nearest help might be over a hundred kilometres away, it pays to be as multi-skilled and as self-sufficient as possible. Investing a bit of time in really getting to know your apps and what they can do is time very well spent indeed.

Conquering Your Inner Luddite with the Right Help

Perhaps one of the best investments of time if you don't have much experience with technology is to do some sort of course in the use of computers and mobile devices. These courses and resources are often free, or low cost because they're run by computer clubs staffed by community-spirited volunteers who enjoy sharing their knowledge and expertise. They are really a godsend to seniors navigating the sometimes-intimidating online world.

There are a number of 'go-to' people for help here: ASCCA, TSS, Be Connected.

ASCCA, the Australian Senior Computer Clubs Association, has over 100 affiliated clubs throughout Australia in every state and territory. We recommend that you join an ASCCA affiliated club near you to take full advantage of membership. A full list of ASCCA-affiliated clubs can be found on their website. Phone: 02 9286 3871; website:

www.ascca.org.au; Email: office@ascca.org.au

As far as ASCCA's reach might be, they're not everywhere, but there are other alternatives where there is no ASCCA club.

Tech Savvy Seniors (TSS) is an initiative of Telstra and is located in New South Wales, Queensland and South Australia. Their website includes free short, self-teach videos and guides in English and some community languages:

www.telstra.com.au/tech-savvy-seniors
www.telstra.com.au/tech-savvy-seniors/language-guides

They also run face-to-face courses through local libraries in English and community languages. See the website for details.

Be Connected is another Australian government initiative that wants 'all Australians to thrive in a digital world'. And it's a great resource to access, especially if you're in a regional or remote region. Who would have thought that there is a computer support club in

Kalgoorlie, Tennant Creek or Aurukun? Go to: **www.beconnected. esafety.gov.au** where you'll find lessons on both Android and Apple mobile devices and an excellent locator map for support clubs.

U3A, the University of the Third Age, is another fantastic resource for seniors. A membership of $30 to $40 per year lets you access a wide variety of courses both in person, and independent study online. If you're the sort of person who prefers to study with others who are at a similar level of (in)competence then you can find others in your local area: **www.u3aonline.org.au/find-a-u3a**

Apps for the Grey Nomad

Aside from the highly recommended FRC app (pages 314 to 318), there are a number of others that you might consider if you have a particular interest in mind. Some are even free!

- AllTrails, a world guide to walking and biking tracks
- Australian Bites and Stings app and First Aid by Australian Red Cross
- Beachsafe
- CamperMate
- Camping Checklist
- Fuel Map Australia
- Mad Paws, for dog-friendly sites and dog-sitters across Australia
- Roadtrippers
- Star Walk 2, for those interested in astronomy
- WIRES Wildlife Rescue, for reporting native animal incidents

Digital Nomads

There's no doubt that if you can learn to use the power of the internet whole new worlds can open up for you and might even lead to viable business that can provide you with nomadic income.

Welcome to the world of the digital nomad. Do a little digging and you'd be surprised at how some nomads have made cyberspace really work for them, especially if you can come up with a product, service, or you have a skill that's in demand. If that's you, then even if you're not in the immediate area when an opportunity arises, people *will* wait for you.

- **www.frc.camp/meetlinda**
- **www.frc.camp/thestringfamily**

Website Resources

Aside from FRC's website and its access to a community of over 100,000 fellow camping enthusiasts, there are a number of other websites from which you can gain some valuable information. As a grey nomad, you can never have too much valuable information.

- **www.atrvc.org.au**
- **www.campermate.com.au/welcome/index**
- **www.freecampingaustralia.com.au**
- **www.goseeaustralia.com.au**
- **www.greynomadsaustralia.com.au**
- **www.greynomadsjobs.com**
- **www.kanguruadventure.com/illegal-camping-in-australia**
- **www.notgreynomads.com**
- **www.thegreynomads.com.au**
- **www.thehub.nrma.com.au**

Food on the Road

Eating is one of many people's favourite subjects. We've already had a few things to say about diet (page 82) but here we'd like to go into a bit of detail about food and cooking in general as a nomad.

Food Storage and Preservation

Not all RVs have refrigeration or freezing, and those that do will require electricity to run them, which might not always be available. When you consider the space limitations that you'll have to deal with then nomads have to rethink the way that they do food.

Consider the following options:

- Dried ingredients, such as nuts, dried fruit and grains are high-density, lightweight foods that you can graze on all the time.
- Leaf vegetables, like Chinese greens and spinach, as well as cauliflower and broccoli, don't store well, so consume them as soon as possible.
- Root vegetables and squashes like pumpkin store for a long time especially in cold conditions, but 'a long time' doesn't mean 'forever' so don't wait until they start sprouting before you consume them.
- Cans are wonderful for wet foods, but they are heavy, so where possible see about buying foods in UHT or Tetra Paks.
- You might be amazed at what you can accomplish with limited utensils. Clever cooks just love sharing their cleverness with other people and if you just ask around, you'll get some great tips. For those of you who like watching videos, we have links to several below to get you inspired.
- If you can, stick to meals that are simple to prepare. This is where a slow cooker might be of great help. The great advantage of slow cooking is that you can buy cheaper but tougher cuts of meats that are more flavoursome, but that lend themselves to long, slow cooking to bring their flavours out and to tenderise them until they melt in your mouth. Slow cooking is also easy, you can just bung in a whole bunch of ingredients in the morning, set and forget, and by evening your meals are ready. Of course, you need a steady supply of power to make this work, but that's what trailer parks and/or solar electricity are for. Slow cooked meals also freeze really easily, so leftovers become the gift that just keeps on giving.
- Alternatively, if you have above-average fire-making and maintaining skills you can cook anywhere that you can get

Take a deep breath and say to yourself, 'Technology is not the enemy. Technology is not the enemy ...'

your hands on firewood, as long as you're not using an open fire at a time or place where there's an extreme fire danger.

- If you're in a town for a while and have made friends and contacts with access to a kitchen, it might pay to make up a whole bunch of meals like curries, soups, stews and the like that can be frozen and reheated in a microwave later.

We'd strongly recommend getting your hands on a copy of an excellent book by Lisa Kathleen Daly, *Healthy Eating for the Time Poor* (New Holland, 2018). The book was written for stressed-out urban parents who want to spend far less time in the kitchen but still give their families nutritious meals, but the principles in the book can be easily applied to nomads who want to spend more time enjoying

Australia and less time cooking but who don't want to compromise too much on flavour and healthy eating. Lisa lived in Kakadu in the Northern Territory and in Monkey Mia in Western Australia for over a year, so she's no stranger to camping and nomadding.

In addition, we've provided some simple recipes for you to get you started (page 210).

Water and Other Drinks

You can never have enough water. In the second driest continent on earth you'll learn to appreciate water in a way that settled people, with their all-too-easy access to town water seldom do. Unless there's a major and unlikely change to human physiology, water will remain the main drink to stay hydrated. After sampling water from all sorts of sources all over the country, you might even become a bit of a water connoisseur.

There are also the other favourites – tea, coffee, soft drinks and the various alcoholic options – but keep this in mind:

- Tea, coffee and alcohol are all diuretic – they make you want to go to the toilet. So however enjoyable they might be to drink, they are actually dehydrating to various extents and some people are more susceptible to dehydration than others.
- Soft drinks tend to make you thirstier because your body needs extra water to metabolise the sugar. Strangely, research has shown that even low or no-sugar ones have a similar effect on your body because your body uses 'sweetness' as a signal to use water in the same way regardless of where the sweetness comes from.
- Remember weight restrictions. You're better off having only a couple of your favourite teas, coffees or other drinks in your RV at a time, and because of storage limitations they won't last as long as they use to before they lose the essential oils that give them their punch. Best to use up your supplies before

buying any more unless you have a particular favourite that is really hard to get and that you can only find in boutique supermarkets in capital cities.

Some Notes About Water and Hygiene

Boondocking, or dry camping, is camping anywhere with limited amenities, including water. In such circumstances water is especially precious and should be reserved for drinking.

You can save water in a number of ways:

- Personal hygiene. Where water is scarce, baby wipes come to the rescue. They're fresh, antibacterial and you'll be amazed how just wiping the 'problem areas' can make you feel really clean.
- Wear loose clothing so grime doesn't build up in between skin and cloth.
- Where possible, bathe in seawater or river water.
- Consider cutting your hair short as shorter hair requires less water to clean. A mixture of one part cornstarch to two parts baking soda makes a natural, somewhat adequate dry shampoo. Just comb in and shake off.
- A mixture of four parts coffee grounds and one part coconut oil vigorously rubbed into the face as a scrub that's then rinsed off with a little water is surprisingly refreshing and leaves you feeling really clean.
- You should also have a water-conserving shower head in your RV if you don't already have one: **www.frc.camp/spatap**
- Dishwashing. Use sand as a pre-wash – this is especially useful in the desert. You'll be amazed how clean you can get dishes just by using clean sand, which acts like steel wool. If you're worried about grit, finish off with a quick rinse.
- Cleaning. Consider using cleaning vinegar in a spray as a way to clean surfaces. The smell doesn't last long in a hot environment.

- If you can, go to the toilet outside. If you have to use an indoor toilet, use the 'If it's yellow let it mellow; If it's brown, flush it down' method of saving on flushes.

Cooking Equipment

Unless you're a raw-food vegan, you're going to have to have some equipment beyond a knife, cutting board and vegetable peeler. We suggest creating a cooking box, where all your equipment is stored in a water- and dust-proof container. The basics are:
- A cook's knife, a cutting board and vegetable peeler
- A wooden spoon, ladle and whisk
- A masher (for mashed potato, pumpkin, sweet potato and the like)
- A meat hammer for tenderising tough cuts (especially important if you're a schnitzel fan)
- A spatula and tongs of various lengths
- A grater for cheese, root vegetables, etc.
- Fold-up or collapsible bucket and sink, for washing up
- Consider a fold-up, heat-resistant cooking pot. They tend to have thin bottoms so they're best used for boiling. Get a good-quality conventional large and another small pot or saucepan for more controlled cooking.
- A set of mixing bowls
- A cast-iron frypan – incredibly versatile and hardy
- Sturdy plates and cutlery
- Tea towels, cling wrap, foil and baking paper
- Oil in spray cans might be more expensive but they are sturdy, keep very well and are much more movement tolerant than oil in bottles.

If you restrict yourself to what you can fit into a large container then that's the basics covered. As we stated above though, if you can organise a slow cooker that also does rice, then you'll have a lot more options.

If you want to go just a little fancier consider getting a convection microwave. They not only act like conventional microwaves but like normal ovens too. They tend to be larger than regular microwaves, but if good food is important to you, they give you a lot more options.

See also

- 'Ultimate Camp Cooking Box Set Up', **www.youtube.com/watch?v=grqQPgd9Q-4.** This is produced by the Seek Adventure YouTube channel that has a lot of useful information.
- 'Kent Survival', which has a whole bunch of videos devoted to bush cooking.

- 'Outdoor Boys', who are American and have great ideas. Check out their video '23 Best Camping Recipes – Basic & Gourmet Meals' – Campfire Meals, **www.youtube.com/watch?v=PDPIfsm52T4**
- 'Overland Travellers' – down-to-earth Australians with an Australian perspective.
- All the recipes that FRC has published to date are available at **www.frc.camp/recipes** recipes and for other camp cooking ideas you might be interested in **www.frc.camp/cookbooks**

There is something tremendously, primally satisfying about campfire cooking even in its most basic form. Still, it pays to be inventive.

Kitchen Essentials

Your pantry and fridge should be stocked with basics that help you with your budget and that you can keep for long periods, preferably without refrigeration.

Eggs are particularly quick, easy and economical to prepare on the road. Nutritious and satisfying, eggs are perfect for breakfast, or for a quick, light meal like an omelette or frittata. Add some bread and a salad for a complete meal.

You can make poached eggs in a microwave in silicone cups you can buy at larger supermarkets or department stores. Feel free to add additional ingredients like tomato or bacon.

Tortillas or tacos are also great for a super-quick and easy meal and you can heat them on a BBQ grill or in a frying pan. You can use tortillas to make wraps for lunchtime using any leftover ingredients or buy a BBQ chook from the supermarket, or add any type of filling you prefer such as mince, chicken, beef or lamb. For vegetarians you can use any vegetables or mixed beans, adding cheese and your favourite sauce or avocado.

Try making quesadillas by filling tortillas with your favourite filling and some cheese and heating on the grill or in the frying pan – dinner will be ready in minutes. Tortillas are also great for making soft tacos. Just heat them up in the microwave or on the grill.

Essentials for the Pantry

- Salt and pepper
- Sugar
- Flour: plain and self-raising
- Breadcrumbs
- Baking powder
- Cereal: oats/muesli/Weet-Bix
- Long life milk

- Your favourite sauces: tomato/BBQ/soy/mustard/ Worcestershire/Tabasco
- Dried herbs and spices
- Tinned foods: tomatoes/baked beans/chick peas/tuna
- Your favourite spreads: honey, jam, peanut butter, Vegemite
- Trail mix, nuts
- Coffee/tea
- Dried pasta and rice
- Instant noodles
- Instant soup
- Tortillas
- Oil: canola/olive oil
- Oil spray
- And anything else you can't live without

Essential Kitchen and BBQ needs

- Cooking knives: larger chef's chopping knife/smaller paring knives
- Cutting board
- Cooking utensils: wooden spoons, flippers, ladle, serving spoons, spatula, whisk, masher, tongs
- Peeler
- Box grater/Microplane-type grater
- Can opener
- Mixing bowls
- Measuring cups and spoons
- Plates and bowls
- Knives, forks, dessertspoons, teaspoons
- Drinking glasses
- Coffee and tea cups
- Bottle opener
- Wine glasses
- Napkins

- Frying pan
- Saucepans (larger for cooking pasta, soup etc, smaller for sauces and reheating)
- Egg rings (silicone)
- Storage Containers for leftovers (square is better for storage)
- Bamboo skewers (for cooking meat/seafood and vegetables on the BBQ or grill
- Scissors
- Tea towels
- Oven mitt
- Dishwashing detergent
- Foil
- Cling wrap
- Paper towel
- Zip-lock bags

If you have space

- Kettle
- Toaster
- Sandwich press
- Grill plates
- Oven trays/muffin trays

Recipes

We've selected these recipes for ease of preparation and because the ingredients are neither difficult to acquire, or expensive. Feel free to tweak or change them to your heart's content, omitting any ingredient that you can't get or that you don't think that you'll like. Cooking should be all about what works for you. Having said that, maybe from time to time be a little daring and take a walk on the wild side.

Please note that you're probably better off buying dried herbs than fresh because they last longer and weigh less. Think about storing them in properly labelled, resealable plastic bags rather than glass jars – that weight thing again.

INSALATA CAPRESE

Serves 4

400 g Roma tomatoes, thickly sliced
240 g bocconcini/fresh mozzarella, sliced
fresh basil leaves, shredded
60 ml extra virgin olive oil
45 ml balsamic vinegar
sea salt and freshly ground black pepper

Arrange tomatoes, bocconcini, and basil leaves on individual plates.

Drizzle with olive oil and balsamic vinegar, and sprinkle with sea salt and freshly ground black pepper.

Serve with crusty bread.

POTATO SALAD WITH BACON & BOILED EGGS

Serves 6

1.5 kg chat potatoes, whole and unpeeled
3 bacon rashers, rind and excess fat removed and diced
185 g sour cream
125 g whole-egg mayonnaise
1 tablespoon wholegrain mustard
1 small red onion, finely diced
1 bunch chives, finely chopped
salt and pepper, to season
4 hard boiled eggs, peeled and quartered
parsley to garnish

Put the potatoes in a large saucepan, cover with water and pinch of salt. Place the saucepan over medium heat and bring to the boil. Reduce the heat and cook the potatoes until tender. Once the potatoes are cooked, drain and let them steam dry. Once cool to the touch, quarter.

Meanwhile, cook the bacon in a frying pan over medium heat until crispy. Remove the bacon from the pan and drain on paper towel.

In a small bowl, mix together the sour cream, mayonnaise, wholegrain mustard, onion and chives.

In a serving bowl, add the potato and combine with the sour cream and mayo mixture. Top with the boiled eggs. Sprinkle with the bacon and parsley.

SWEET COLESLAW

Makes 2–3 cups

1 small head cabbage, finely chopped
2 carrots, peeled and grated
1 red/Spanish onion, finely sliced

Dressing
1 cup whole egg mayonnaise
¼ cup apple cider
3 tablespoons sugar
salt and pepper, to taste

In a large bowl, combine the cabbage, carrot and onion. In a separate bowl, mix the mayonnaise, cider and sugar and season to taste.

Add the dressing to the cabbage and coat well. Refrigerate until required.

BRUSCHETTA

Serves 4

8 Roma or plum tomatoes, roughly chopped
1 medium red onion, finely chopped
10 basil leaves, chopped
salt, to taste
20 ml olive oil
30 ml balsamic dressing
1 baguette
1 large clove garlic, slightly crushed
105 g butter
120 g fresh goats cheese

In a bowl, combine the tomatoes, onion, basil leaves, salt, oil and balsamic dressing.

Cut the baguette into diagonal slices, rub with garlic and spread with butter. Place on a hot BBQ grill and cook until golden brown.

Serve the tomato mix and goats cheese on the hot garlic bread. The tomato mix is good if prepared a few hours in advance.

AVOCADO DIP

Serve with corn chips, crackers or vegetables

1 large avocado
½ cup sour cream
¼ cup oil
3 tablespoons lemon juice
½ teaspoons sugar
¼ teaspoons garlic salt
dash of Tabasco sauce if desired
salt to taste

It's best to blend all the ingredients in a food processor but when on the road you can mix all the ingredients together in a mixing bowl and mash with a fork until it has formed more of a dip consistency.

Add salt to taste.

TOMATO AND CHEESE DIP

This tasty dip is substantial enough to be served with corn chips or crackers and strips of raw vegetables as a light meal.

300 g jar of tomato salsa (which can be bought or make your own with chopped tomatoes and thinly sliced onions, adding salt and pepper to taste)

2 teaspoons cornflour

1½ cups of grated mild cheese, preferably mozzarella

Place the salsa in a medium-sized pot on medium/high. When just about to boil, mix the cornflour to a paste in a tablespoon of cold water. Add this to the salsa and heat until the mixture boils and thickens.

Stir in the grated cheese, remove from heat and leave to stand until the cheese begins to melt. Reheat before serving if necessary.

Note: For more heat, add 1 teaspoon of chilli powder or 1 teaspoon of hot chilli sauce.

POTATO WEDGES

Serves 4

4–6 medium-sized washed potatoes
1 teaspoon freshly crushed garlic
4 teaspoons finely chopped rosemary
60 ml olive oil
90 ml fresh lemon juice
½ teaspoon pepper
salt, to taste

Halve the potatoes then cut each half into 4–6 wedges. Place into a large bowl. Mix the garlic, rosemary, oil and lemon juice together, pour over potatoes and toss well to coat. Sprinkle with pepper.

Cook over direct heat in a covered BBQ. Cook for 20 minutes, turning the potatoes after 10 minutes. Cook until tender and crisp. The dish can be moved to indirect heat while other dishes finish cooking. To serve, sprinkle lightly with salt.

CORN ON THE COB

Serves 4

4 cobs of corn
30 g butter, melted, plus extra to serve
salt and freshly ground black pepper, to taste

Pull back the husks and strip the silk off the corn, retaining the husks. Brush the corn with melted butter and sprinkle with salt and freshly ground black pepper. Replace the husks and secure in three places with string.

Barbecue the corn cobs over a hot grill for 15–20 minutes, or until tender, turning frequently. When cooked, the husks will be dry and brown and the corn will be golden brown. Serve with melted butter and salt and pepper.

BALSAMIC VEGETABLES

Serves 6

2 large zucchini (courgette)
1 red capsicum (pepper)
1 yellow capsicum (pepper)
1 green capsicum (pepper)
3 beetroot
1 large eggplant (aubergine)
2 red onions
45 ml balsamic vinegar
2 garlic cloves, crushed
10 g thyme
10 g basil
60 ml olive oil
balsamic glaze

Cut all the vegetables to equal size and place in a foil barbecue roasting tray lined with baking paper.

Combine the balsamic vinegar, garlic, thyme, basil and oil in a bowl and whisk. Add the dressing to the vegetables and toss to coat.

Place the tray on a medium–high BBQ grill and close the lid. Roast, tossing every 5–10 minutes, until golden and tender.

Dress with the balsamic glaze and serve.

GRILLED ASPARAGUS

2 bunches asparagus
60 ml olive oil
salt and pepper, to season
balsamic glaze

Snap off the woody part of the asparagus, then toss in the olive oil and season with salt and pepper.

Cook the asparagus on a medium-hot BBQ grill for 2-3 minutes, then turn over and cook for a further 2-3 minutes or until charred and tender.

Serve on a platter and drizzle with balsamic glaze just before serving.

VEGO OMELETTE

Serves 2

3–4 large eggs
2 tablespoons milk
pinch black pepper
½ red onion, sliced
1 tablespoon olive oil
handful of cherry tomatoes
½ cup fresh baby spinach leaves
2 tablespoons crumbled feta or your favourite cheese

In a small bowl, whisk eggs, milk and pepper.

In a frying pan, sauté red onion in oil until soft, then add tomato. Cook for 2 minutes then transfer to a plate and set aside. Pour the egg mixture into the hot pan, then spoon onion, tomato, spinach and feta into the middle of the cooking egg mixture. Cover, reduce to medium heat and cook for 4–5 minutes or until spinach is wilted.

Uncover, fold the omelette in half and serve.

RUM AND BARBECUE SAUCE

1 teaspoon olive oil
1 small onion, finely grated
2 garlic cloves, crushed
240 ml tomato sauce
20 ml soy sauce
1 teaspoon mustard powder
60 g brown sugar
120 ml spiced rum

Add the oil, onion and garlic to a small saucepan over medium heat and cook until the onion is transparent.

Add all the remaining ingredients, except the rum, and bring to the boil. Simmer for 20 minutes. Remove from the heat, then add the rum and stir. Allow to cool.

Note: Store in an airtight container in the fridge for 1–2 weeks.

GARLIC MAYONNAISE

Makes $\frac{3}{4}$ cup

¾ cup whole egg mayonnaise
2 tablespoons Greek yoghurt
1 teaspoon lemon juice
1 tablespoon parsley, finely chopped
1 garlic clove, minced

Whisk the ingredients together in a small bowl. Cover with cling wrap then refrigerate until ready to use.

STICKY CHICKEN DRUMETTES

Serves 4–6

1 kg chicken drumettes
60 ml soy sauce
60 ml barbecue sauce
60 ml honey
1 garlic clove, crushed
1 teaspoon salt
½ teaspoon ground pepper

Place the drumettes in a large zip lock bag. Add the remaining ingredients and shake the bag to coat the drumettes. Refrigerate until needed.

Preheat the BBQ grill to medium–high heat. Cook the drumettes for 15–20 minutes, or until golden brown, crispy and completely cooked through. Keep basting the chicken with the marinade throughout the cooking process. If the drumettes begin to burn, move the wings to a cooler part of the grill or reduce the heat.

Remove from the BBQ and place on a platter to serve.

BUTTERFLIED LEMON CHICKEN

Serves 2–4

1.2–1.5 kg whole chicken, cut through the backbone
45 ml Worcestershire sauce
salt
½ teaspoon cracked black pepper
1 garlic clove, crushed
juice and zest of 1 lemon
olive oil

Put the chicken on a chopping board, breast side down, and using a pair of kitchen scissors, cut through each side of the backbone.

Turn the chicken breast side up and open the chicken. Place your hand on top and flatten. Rub the chicken with the Worcestershire sauce, salt, pepper, garlic, lemon and olive oil.

Place the chicken on the BBQ grill, breast side down, and cook over a medium–high heat for 15–20 minutes, depending on size. Turn and cook for a further 15–20 minutes.

Cook until the chicken is just cooked through rest covered for 5 mins then serve.

Note: Cover chicken and let marinate in fridge for at least 1 hour and up to 8 hours.

STICKY BEER CAN CHICKEN

Serves 6

1 large whole chicken
1 teaspoon vegetable oil
¼ teaspoon pepper
½ teaspoon sea salt
½ teaspoon chicken spice rub
1 can beer (or soda can may also be used)
45 ml barbecue sauce

Pat down the chicken with a paper towel to absorb any moisture. Rub the chicken inside and out with vegetable oil. Season with salt, pepper and spice rub.

Open the beer can and pour out half of the liquid. Place the can on a cutting board and lower the chicken onto the can so it looks like it is sitting on it. Position the legs like a tripod so the chicken sits upright.

Prepare the BBQ for indirect cooking. Place the chicken in the middle of the BBQ and close lid. Cook the chicken for about an hour or until golden brown.

The chicken is done when the juices run clear when a skewer is pushed into the thickest part of the thigh. Brush the chicken with barbecue sauce and cook for a further 10 minutes until dark and sticky.

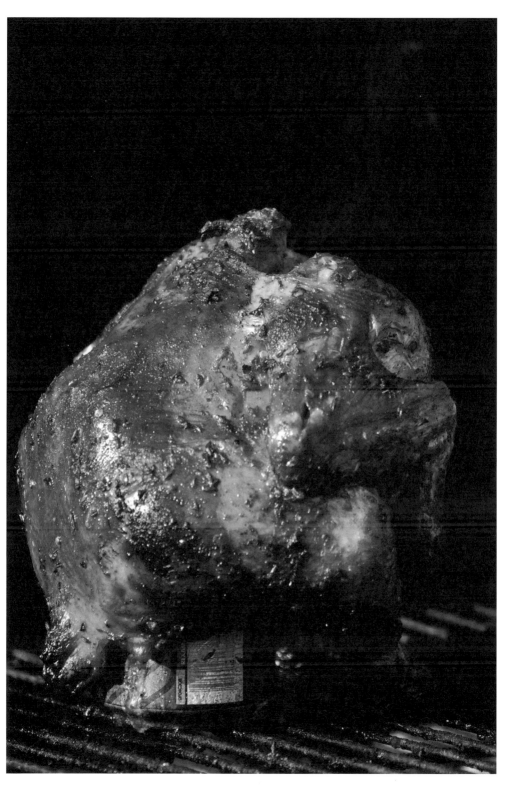

LOLLYPOP CHICKEN STICKS

Serves 4

500 g ground chicken meat
½ cup breadcrumbs
1 medium onion, peeled
½ teaspoon salt
2 tablespoons chopped fresh parsley
½ teaspoon pepper
2 tablespoons lemon juice
oil
20 mini bamboo skewers, soaked in water for 20 minutes

Place the chicken in a bowl. Add the breadcrumbs. Using fine side of a grater, grate the onion over the breadcrumbs to catch the juice. Add all remaining ingredients except the oil. Mix and knead well with your hands to combine and make the chicken mix fine. Allow to stand for 15 minutes.

With wet hands take a portion of chicken and mould around the stick to a 35 mm length. Arrange on an oiled tray, cover and refrigerate for 1 hour.

Prepare the BBQ for medium–hot direct-heat cooking. Oil the grill and place the chicken sticks on it. Cook for 10–12 minutes, or until cooked through, turning frequently. Serve hot.

BARBECUE MEATBALL SKEWERS

Serves 4-6

oil, for cooking
1 onion, finely diced
500 g beef mince
1 egg
2 bacon rashers, finely diced
20 ml barbecue sauce
20 ml Worcestershire sauce
1 garlic clove, crushed
45 g fine breadcrumbs
salt and black pepper, to season

If using bamboo skewers, soak in water for 20 minutes.

Heat some oil in a frying pan over medium heat. Add the bacon and the onion then cook until the onion is soft and golden. Combine the remaining ingredients, ensuring they are well mixed, then roll into golf size balls.

Place four balls on each skewer. Place the skewers on a medium–high BBQ flatplate and cook for 8–12 minutes or until golden brown, turning every few minutes to brown all sides.

Serve with salad and coleslaw or place the meatballs on a long bread roll.

STEAK WITH PEPPER SAUCE

Serves 4

500 g rump steak, trimmed
freshly ground black pepper

Pepper sauce
knob of butter
½ cup fresh parsley, chopped
½ cup fresh chives, chopped
¼ cup cream
salt, to taste

\\

Place the rump steak on the BBQ grill on high heat and lightly sprinkle with pepper. Cook until lightly browned, then turn and lightly sprinkle the other side with pepper.

To make the sauce, melt the butter in a pan and fry the herbs, then add the cream. If you want a lot of sauce, add all the cream. If only a little sauce is required, add only half the quantity.

Serve the rump steak with sauce on the side, season with salt to taste.

SKIRT STEAK SATAYS

Serves 4

1 skirt steak or flank, about 700 g
2 tablespoons oil
1 tablespoon lime or lemon juice
salt and pepper to taste
½ cup satay sauce
juice of ½ lemon
1 tablespoon peanut oil
20 long satay sticks, soaked for 30 minutes in cold water

Place the skirt steak on a chopping board. Remove any membrane. With a large knife lightly score the surface in a diagonal criss-cross pattern on both sides. This has a tenderising effect as it cuts through the meat fibres; it also speeds up absorption of the marinade.

Mix the oil, lime juice, salt and pepper together. Place the steak in a flat, non-metallic dish. Pour in the oil mixture, turn the meat to coat both sides. Marinate for 2 hours, turning once. Remove from the marinade, pat dry and place on a cutting board. Slice the steak across the grain, with knife held at a 45-degree angle to the meat. Strips should be about 12 cm long, 2 cm wide and 3 mm thick.

Weave the strips onto the soaked satay sticks and gently spread them out flat, not bunched up. Arrange the skewers in a non-metallic flat dish, a lasagna dish for example. Combine the lemon juice, satay sauce and peanut oil to form a marinade. Pour over the skewers. Marinate for 30 minutes.

Prepare the BBQ for direct-heat cooking on high heat. Oil the grill bars well. Slip a double foil band under the exposed part of the skewers to protect them from burning. Arrange the satay sticks and cook for 1–2 minutes per side. Serve immediately with extra satay sauce.

SMOKY BARBECUE SPARE RIBS

Serves 6–8

2 x 1 kg racks ribs
120 ml olive oil
Rum and Barbecue Sauce – see page 235

Place the ribs in a large, zip lock bag. Thoroughly combine the Rum and Barbecue sauce and the oil and pour onto the ribs.

Marinate in the refrigerator for several hours or overnight, turning occasionally.

Take two large sheets of heavy-duty foil and place on a work surface. Place a rack of ribs on each. Generously cover both sides of ribs with extra marinade. Wrap into a double-folded parcel, making sure all joins are well sealed to prevent leakage. Carefully place the parcel onto a tray, taking care not to tear the foil. Refrigerate if not cooking immediately.

Prepare the BBQ for direct-heat cooking. Place a wire cake rack on the grill bars to stand 2.5 cm (1 in) above the grill. Place the foil parcels on the rack and cook for 10 minutes on each side, a total of 20 minutes. Move the parcel to a plate. Open the foil and discard. Lift the ribs onto the rack. Continue cooking and brush with extra relish, turning until ribs are well browned and crisp, this should take about 10 minutes. Cut between the ribs to separate, pile onto a platter and serve immediately.

You must eat these as soon as they are cooked otherwise they will become dry and tough.

LEG OF LAMB

Serves 4

1 ½ kg boneless leg of lamb, butterflied
½ cup fresh rosemary leaves, roughly chopped
1 tablespoon salt
½ teaspoon black pepper, freshly ground
½ teaspoon coriander powder
½ teaspoon mild Indian curry powder
olive oil

Lay the leg of lamb out as flat as possible and ensure that the meat has an even thickness. This can be difficult as the muscle structure varies and so you may have to slice the meat to flatten it. Skewer into place to maintain a flat appearance.

Mix the rosemary, salt, pepper, coriander and curry powder together. With your fingers, sprinkle/spread half the rub ingredients over the cut side of the lamb and then massage it in.

Put the leg of lamb onto a medium–hot BBQ grill cut-side down. Cook for five minutes.

Lightly brush the skin side of the lamb with oil and turn the leg over to cook for 10–15 minutes with the hood down.

Brush the partially cooked cut side with a little oil and sprinkle over the remaining rub. Turn the meat over again, drop the hood, and leave to cook for 10–15 minutes.

Turn the leg one more time to the open flesh side and cook for a further 10–15 minutes with the hood down. When cooked to your liking remove from the BBQ and let it rest for 5 minutes. Slice the meat and serve with salads or vegetables of your choice.

LAMB RISSOLES

Serves 6

500 g lamb mince
1 small onion finely diced
½ cup breadcrumbs
¼ bunch fresh mint, finely chopped (keep some for garnish)
1 clove garlic finely chopped
1 teaspoon ground cumin
salt and pepper
¼ cup diced sweet chargrilled capsicum (available in jars at the supermarket)
1 egg
spray oil for cooking

Place the mince, onion, breadcrumbs, mint, garlic and cumin in the bowl and combine. Add sweet chargrilled capsicum and egg. Season with salt and pepper.

Divide mince mixture into 6 portions then shape each portion into a patty.

Heat BBQ plate or chargrill over medium–low heat. Spray both sides of rissoles with oil. Cook, turning occasionally, for 12–15 minutes or until cooked through.

Serve on platter or make a burger.

CHORIZO & BOCCONCINI SKEWERS

Makes 12

12 skewers, either steel or bamboo (if bamboo soak in water for 20 minutes so they don't burn)

1 large chorizo sausage

12 small basil leaves

12 small bocconcini balls

6 cherry tomatoes, halved or whole depending on what you like (one piece of tomato per skewer)

finely ground black pepper

Slice chorizo into 12 pieces and pan-fry or grill on the BBQ for 2–4 minutes or until cooked and the edges are starting to crisp. Set aside on paper towel to cool slightly.

Thread a basil leaf onto a skewer, then a bocconcini ball, a tomato half then a slice of chorizo finished with a sprinkle of pepper to taste.

BARBECUED MUSSELS WITH CHILLI LIME DRESSING

Serves 4–6

1 kg mussels
fresh chives for garnish

Chilli Lime Dressing
1 clove garlic, crushed and finely chopped
¼ cup fresh lime juice
1 tablespoon Thai fish sauce
½ teaspoon prepared minced chilli
½ teaspoon brown sugar

Rinse mussels under cool running water, scrubbing the outside and debearding the mussels if needed, pull the fibrous beard towards the hinge of the shell to remove.

Preheat the BBQ hotplate and place the mussels on top. Cook until the mussels open, covering if you have a lidded barbecue.

Discard any mussels that do not open. Break off and discard the top shell of the cooked mussels.

For the chilli lime dressing, mix the garlic, lime juice, fish sauce, chilli and brown sugar together.

Arrange the mussels on a platter and drizzle the dressing over them. Garnish with chives.

MUSSELS MARINIÈRES

Serves 4

1 kg mussels
1 small onion, sliced
1 clove garlic, chopped
¼ cup white wine
freshly ground black pepper
¼ cup parsley, chopped
15 g butter

Rinse mussels under cool running water, scrubbing the outside and debearding the mussels if needed, pull the fibrous beard towards the hinge of the shell to remove.

In a large saucepan heat butter over medium–high heat.

When butter starts to foam, add onions and garlic. Stir and cook until onions are transparent and garlic is soft, about 2–3 minutes.

Add wine, stir to combine.

Add the cleaned mussels to the pot, cover, and steam for 2–3 minutes until the mussels have just opened. Discarding any mussels which remain closed.

Transfer to serving dishes and pour over the liquid or leave in the pan to serve, season with pepper as desired and garnish with parsley. Serve with crusty bread.

Note: You can buy mussels ready to cook, scrubbed and debearded from most supermarkets.

GRILLED SALMON WITH GARLIC LEMON BUTTER

Serves 6

120 g unsalted butter
4 cloves garlic, smashed
1 teaspoon salt
¼ teaspoon black pepper
45 ml fresh lemon or lime juice, plus wedges to serve
fresh dill or parsley, chopped, plus more to garnish
1 kg salmon skin on, cut into 6 fillets

Melt butter over medium heat. Smash garlic cloves with the flat of a large knife and add to butter along with salt and pepper. Cook for a couple of minutes, or until fragrant. Add lemon juice and chopped herbs then remove from heat.

Transfer half of sauce to a small bowl. Reserve and set aside remaining sauce in the pan – you will use this for serving. Arrange salmon fillets on a platter skin-side down and brush tops with 1/2 of the sauce from the bowl. Let salmon marinate in refrigerator for 15 minutes.

Preheat grill to medium–high. Brush the hot grill clean and oil the grates. Place salmon onto preheated grill, skin-side down. Cover and grill undisturbed, about 2 minutes on the first side. Carefully flip salmon over, cover and cook another 2 minutes. Flip again and brush tops with the remaining sauce. Continue grilling until salmon is flaky and cooked through (approx. another 1 minute). Remove salmon from grill and drizzle with reserved sauce.

Garnish with fresh herbs and serve with lemon or lime wedges to squeeze over salmon if desired.

GRILLED FLATHEAD

Serves 4

flathead, whole
4 tablespoons olive oil
2 tablespoons cajun spice
2 lemons
bunch of fresh dill or parsley
wooden skewers, soaked for 20 minutes

Ask the fishmonger to clean and gut the fish. Cut off the fins and trim the tail with a pair of kitchen scissors. In a small bowl mix together the olive oil and the cajun spice. Slice the lemons. Wash the herbs and trim off the stalks.

Fill the fish cavity with a good handful of herbs and 2–3 slices of lemon, then pour on some of the oil and spice mix. With 2–3 small wooden skewers, fasten together the fish so herbs and lemon do not fall out during cooking.

Turn the fish over and rub the oil and spice mix into the fish well.

Prepare the BBQ for direct-heat cooking. Oil the grill bars well. Cook the fish on each side for 8–10 minutes. Serve with mixed salad.

Note: If you can't get flathead use snapper or your favourite fish.

FISH KEBABS

Serves 4

800 g fish, cubed
bamboo skewers (presoaked in water)

Marinade
2 cloves garlic, finely chopped
1 small red chilli, finely chopped
pinch sea salt
½ lemon, juiced
240 ml olive oil

Thread fish cubes onto skewers.

Combine all marinade ingredients.

Place kebabs in a baking dish and cover with marinade. Refrigerate, turning occasionally, for 15 minutes.

Heat BBQ to medium-high. Cook on a BBQ plate or in a baking dish or grill for approximately 10–15 minutes depending on the type of fish you use, until fish is cooked.

PART FIVE

THE ART OF CAMPING AND NOMADDING

///

The Art of Camping

There are rules for camping that are common for all camping situations, whether you're staying at a paid campsite or roughing it in the wild.

Respect the environment. Australia is a big place but it's not a garbage can for your waste products. Cities and towns have all sorts of ways of handling human-generated waste, but once you're outside any main population centre, you're actually in the home of millions of animal and plant species and they deserve your consideration.

The general rule is: take out what you bring in. If you generate garbage wait until you are in an appropriate place to get rid of it. This includes black wastewater.

Keep control of your fires. Remember that bushfires can start with the smallest of sparks or carelessly tossed cigarette butts and can cause millions of dollars damage and cost lives. Make sure that you thoroughly put out any fires you start.

Respect other people. Being in the wild is not a licence to abandon the rules of civilised conduct. We're probably preaching to the choir here. A more likely scenario is that you'll be the victim of bad behaviour rather than the cause of it. Be aware that there are authorities to whom you should report bad behaviour so that it doesn't continue. The nomad community is a small town, and word gets around pretty quickly about who's a troublemaker.

Free Camping or Paid Camping?

With over 9000 campsites dotted around Australia the choices for nomads are effectively endless. The principle of where to stay is pretty much the same as the principle of real estate – location, location, location. If you want to be in or close to a particular place, that defines your choices. However, in many cases there's more than one option. At this point you need to know:

The rules of camping include reading signs and doing what they ask you to do.

- Is the campsite free or paid? Paid campsites in Australia generally range in price from $20–60 per night. National Park fees are around $10–15 per day per vehicle.
- Like everything else the price of a campsite is determined by supply and demand and, naturally, what amenities the campsite offers. Expect to pay a premium for sites that have power, water and decent laundry and showering facilities in the best locations.
- Is the campsite animal friendly?
- Is the campsite child friendly? It's rare that they aren't, but some campsites have more of a 'family vibe' than others and you might need to trust your gut here.

With over 9000 campsites throughout Australia to choose from this is where technology really comes into its own. Your best friend here is the FRC app, which gives you addresses, contact details and up-to-date information about campsites at any location on the continent.

'Free camp' doesn't mean 'shabby camp' but it does mean that facilities are limited. Free camp at Renmark South Australia along the Murray River.

Remember to look out for rules like vehicle size restrictions before you consider going to a particular caravan park. It's always best to phone ahead to check for opening times and availability.

National and State Parks

Visiting national and state parks is an activity subject to certain conditions. The best source of information about these parks is to go directly to the websites as entry is often restricted in an effort to conserve the environment, bookings are required, and there are entry fees involved. You can book entry to the parks through the sites too. Parks Australia is responsible for six national parks – Booderee, Christmas Island, Kakadu, Norfolk Island, Pulu Keeling, Norfolk Island, Uluru-Kata Tjuta – as well as 58 marine parks and the Australian National Botanic Gardens in Canberra; **www.parksaustralia.gov.au**

By state or territory the responsible bodies are:

Commercial or paid campsites pretty much reflect the area you find them in. This one's the BIG4 holiday park in Wagga Wagga, NSW.

The Australian Capital Territory: Namadgi National Park, **www. environment.act.gov.au/parks-conservation/parks-and-reserves/find-a-park/namadgi-national-park/namadgi-national-park**

New South Wales: **www.nationalparks.nsw.gov.au**

South Australia: **www.parks.sa.gov.au/Home**

Tasmania: **www.parks.tas.gov.au**

The Northern Territory: **www.nt.gov.au/leisure/parks-reserves/find-a-park/find-a-park-to-visit**

Queensland: **www.qpws.usedirect.com/QPWS**

Victoria: **www.parkweb.vic.gov.au**

Western Australia: **www.parks.dpaw.wa.gov.au**

NOTE: It might seem strange to some that authorities can close an entire national park, but the reasons are sound. Some parts of Australia at some times of the year are simply too dangerous to travel in.

Lake Conjola, NSW.

Etiquette

Here are some basic rules of caravan park, campsite etiquette that will ensure you are the sort of camper who is welcome anywhere, not one who, at the very least, will be complained about or, at worst, will be evicted or banned.

- First up, read the rules. Ignorance of the park or site rules is no excuse and abiding by them is a condition of entry. Find out what the boundaries are and respect them.
- Be polite. Friendliness doesn't mean smiling at everyone all the time, nor does it mean saying 'hello' to everyone and forcing them to respond. After all, they might be deep in thought and your 'hello' might be an unwanted intrusion into their mindspace. However, politeness does mean that if someone communicates with you in a civil manner you respond with equal civility.
- Cleanliness. Don't create messes for others to clean up. 'Messes' include leaving untidy showers or unwelcome deposits in toilet bowls.
- Give feedback. Unless the people running the campsites are idiots (and unfortunately, some of them are, stupidity tends to show up pretty quickly in the bush), they'll want to know when they're doing a good job or a bad job. Let the proprietors or management know about any concerns or problems that arise during your stay. Certainly, let them know about any potential or actual dangers to people or property. And don't be scant with praise if you've had a great time. People like positive feedback too.
- Keep noise to a minimum. There are morning people and night owls, both should respect the other's circadian rhythms. Newsflash! Generators are noisy! So only use them during times and under conditions allowed for at the site. Remember

they're not even allowed in national parks and if you get caught using one the park ranger will fine you.

- Kids. Keep them on a short leash (figuratively) in crowded areas. Like pets, not everyone is a fan of children, especially at 6.00 am.
- Lighting. Don't leave your exterior lights on all night. If necessary, use a timer. Light pollution is definitely a thing if people want to sleep or even if they simply want to enjoy the heavens.
- Respect personal space. This includes the invisible border around your RV rig, so place your rig as close to the centre of your allocated space as possible. Don't walk through another camper's allocated space or site. If you do accidently, and the opportunity presents itself, apologise. And don't park your rig where you restrict another camper's ability to access their RV or to leave the campsite.
- Respect the wildlife. Don't feed the wildlife, either actively, or passively by leaving food scraps around. Don't harass the wildlife with intrusions into their space.

Low cost campsite Jugoing, NSW.

- Return the stuff. Anything that belongs to the site that you borrow or use should be returned to its designated space – clean!
- Wash your dishes in the camp kitchen. Do not wash your dishes in the bathroom or shower block.

The rules of campsite etiquette are there to ensure that strangers living in close proximity to each other don't end up wanting to commit various forms of homicide after arriving somewhere following a long journey.

More Thinking Outside the Box: Camping at Properties – Negotiations, Etiquette and Contingencies

There's nothing stopping you from negotiating directly with property owners to see if you can stay on their property. Many, in fact, even invite this and advertise for potential stayers. FRC has dedicated classified ad categories for house or farm sitting where you can negotiate to stay on someone's property with your RV and look after it when they are not there: **www.frc.camp/sitting**

FRC also has a Help Out section for cases where you can stay on the property in exchange for accommodation and services when the owners are still at home: **www.frc.camp/helpingout**. Make sure that you clarify the following:

- When can you stay? When do you need to leave by?
- Do you have the use of any buildings on the property?
- Are you free to use other amenities like internet access, food in storage etc?
- Are there any specific things you need to do, like look after pets, do repair or maintenance jobs, etc?
- Have the property owners provided you with emergency contact details?
- Have they informed their neighbours of what's going on?

Many people who enter into these arrangements find the experiences rewarding and, as a bonus, they make new friends. Given the opportunity, who wouldn't want to negotiate a stay at a real country property, and make new friends in the process?

Glamping

Glamour camping, or glamping, is a recent phenomenon, which tries to give you an outdoorsy, camping experience with a touch (often a big touch) of luxury. Quite a number of glamping experiences have become available in Australia in recent years for those who want a booster shot of creature comforts.

For an introduction to the world of glamping, visit:
www.australia.com/en/things-to-do/accommodation-and-places-to-stay/australias-best-glamping-experiences.html

Life on the Water

Although it's not a hugely popular option because of Australia's limited number of available waterways there might be a future for you on the water. Maybe nomadding in a houseboat would be right for you? This isn't something you're going to want to rush into and we're really only introducing you to the idea to be provocative, but if there's one thing that nomadding does better than anything else it's exposing you to locals, people and lifestyles that you otherwise wouldn't see and that generally aren't highlighted in the media. So, while you're RVing all over the place you might occasionally stop at a river or in a sheltered inlet or bay and see what living on a houseboat might be like.

There are a number of places throughout Australia where you could make this work. Among them, the Murray River is ideal. Living there in the long term might also inspire you to lobby the government for better management of our river systems.

What the Travel Guides Don't Always Tell You

Dealing with ageism, racism, sexism or any other 'ism'

It's rare, but every now and then you'll come across people whose attitude to our cultural and lifestyle diversity is, shall we say, unenlightened. How you deal with this is up to you, but our advice is that it's a big country, so often it's just best to walk away; there are plenty of other people and places that will welcome you with open arms.

However, once you know how to use social media you can always use this as a platform to tell your story. Stick to the facts about what happened during a negative incident, not your feelings about it or your interpretation. People are smart enough to read between the lines and if a business or individual is involved and word spreads, they'll soon get their karmic backlash.

Misinformation

Sometimes information about a location or a business or service is out of date or misleading. That's why there are forums to discuss these things. Make use of the power of these forums. FRC's website and

app are being constantly updated, so that minimises the possibility of out-of-date information, but misleading information is somewhat harder to police without invoking the power of the people. FRC has a variety of different mechanisms where members can disseminate or update information to other members.

Random Visitors

From time to time people might invade your space and enter your RV. In most cases this is accidental; people can get confused or distracted, especially at night. However, if the situation is more serious you need to prepare for it. If you feel vulnerable carry a panic alarm. It's better to look stupid or embarrassed in the case of a false alarm or misunderstanding than to end up on the receiving end of trespass or assault. We hate to say this, but wildlife and natural disasters aren't the only things that can potentially harm you in Australia. There are, unfortunately, nutcases out there and though you might never encounter them it's best to take some basic precautions.

- A satellite phone (page 186) will enable you to contact authorities. Even if the authorities are a long way away, it's better than nothing.
- Where possible, inform somebody responsible about where you're going, when you plan to arrive and when you plan to return from your destination. That way if you're inordinately late someone will have raised even a tentative 'yellow alert' that you might be in trouble.
- Never, ever, ever approach the scene of what looks like an accident or incident without first attempting to contact authorities. Resist that first impulse to help. It's much better to raise a minor false alarm and look a little silly, or to get some advice about how to deal with something than to find yourself in some sort of situation that you can't get out of.

Things That Want to Bite and Kill You

Australia has a reputation for having deadly wildlife. This is unfair and everywhere on planet Earth has some animal or plant that is potentially lethal. In any case, the best thing to do is take some elementary precautions:
- Don't underestimate the value of mosquito and fly netting. In some places this simple protection will save your sanity.
- Don't skimp on protective clothing if you're going to be anywhere near things that can sting you, including plants.
- Learn about any potentially dangerous wildlife from the local authorities in the area that you're visiting. The good news is that in the vast majority of cases animals are happy to be left alone and will only attack you if you provoke them, so don't.
- It might be an idea to carry an EpiPen and learn how to use it. You don't want to wait until you're stung by an insect to learn that you're actually severely allergic and could die from anaphylactic shock.

Respecting the local wildlife doesn't mean that from time to time they won't ingress on 'your' territory. And while they might look cute, there's a whole range of animals who are perfectly capable of injuring you if, for whatever reason, they feel threatened, or even if they're rather too enthusiastic in their sense of fun. As always, we advise caution.

The Snob Factor

This is a problem that's more comical than serious, but you might find that there's a certain snobbery attached to certain rigs and you'll notice this if your humble van doesn't quite live up to someone else's five-star mobile home. Shrug it off. People who judge you on how much money you've spent on your rig are dealing with insecurity issues and they deserve some psychotherapy. They certainly don't deserve your attention. There's also reverse snobbery, where people feel inadequate because your 'stuff' is better than theirs. This again, is more a reflection of their insecurities than yours. In the end the only thing that matters is that you've made choices that work for *you*. You're not responsible for how other people choose to feel, after all.

Helping Out Regional Australia

One thing that nomads can do is by their very presence they can help out communities throughout regional Australia. There are lots of ways to help, including:

- Volunteering to help at events in exchange for accommodation
- Getting involved in the local community, especially if you plan to stay a while
- Starting some sort of initiative, especially if you have a much-needed skill in demand.

It all depends on what level of involvement you want and how much you want to invest in a place. Remember that advice about a long-term bolthole we mentioned on page 54? If you really like a particular place then making yourself useful around town is not only great for your mental and physical health and wellbeing, it also generates a lot of goodwill in a community that might one day be your permanent home.

For some inspiring stories about how helping out is a win/win for all involved visit:

www.frc.camp/help@margaretriver
www.frc.camp/help@thomasbrookwines
www.frc.camp/outbacklinks

Not Grey Nomads

Frannie and 'Crispy' Chris are in their forties and in 2017 decided that a life on the road with their furbaby (American Staffordshire terrier and Labrador cross) Bella was for them.

Visit their website and read their blog for a different point of view from people who didn't want to wait until they were grey to embark on a life of nomadic adventure: **www.notgreynomads.com**

The Big Lap

There is an adage that many nomads go by when it comes to travelling in the Top End: in by Mother's Day; out by Father's Day. Essentially, in by early May; out by early September. This annual movement to take advantage of the four-month window of opportunity to get the best of the north before oppressive heat or the rainy season sets in is popularly known as the grey nomad migration. Many tend to move into the northern parts of Queensland, across the Northern Territory and then into Western Australia – either clockwise (west to east) or anti-clockwise (east to west). During this period the roads are more congested and you have to get into your campsite quite early as many will fill fast. The take home lesson here is plan ahead and, if you can, pay a security deposit to guarantee your place.

But Australia is a big place. It would take more than a lifetime to explore it fully, so, to help you prioritise, aside from The Big Lap (page 159), we've compiled a short list of highlights for each state and territory.

The Australian Capital Territory

The ACT is not exactly a nomad favourite, apart from the obvious landmarks. For most people the ACT is synonymous with Canberra, and the War Memorial is on everyone's list, as is Parliament House, both the new and the old. The Mint is worth a look and Lake Burley Griffin is very nice. Questacon, the National Science and Technology Centre, is a lot of fun, but noisy. The National Library is interesting and quiet. Mount Ainslie Lookout gives a nice view of the lake and Parliament House. There's also **Namadgi National Park** and the surrounding districts. There's a surprising amount to see and do in Canberra and the ACT.

Canberra is full of more 'human focused' activities if the gorgeous natural wonders that the rest of Australia has to offer begin to get too much for you.

New South Wales

When it comes to New South Wales, focus on areas that you can base yourself in, rather than specific iconic sites. Of course, there is **Sydney** and the harbour; **the Blue Mountains** and the Three Sisters and all that but there are also some great towns and other locations worth a look. **The Hunter Valley** is always a popular place, especially for wine buffs, and there are a few free camps in the smaller towns that allow you to stay and explore. Near to Sydney, **Jenolan Caves** are very popular with nomads. Access can be a bit tricky depending on the size of rigs so it's probably best to stay in outlying areas such as Lithgow then make the drive there for the day. The **Dubbo** area is popular because of the Western Plains Zoo – quite a few wildlife-loving nomads make that trip. And **Lightning Ridg**e is popular for opal lovers. **Broken Hill** is, surprisingly, a very popular destination, in spite of its isolation, but nomads are well catered for, with plenty to do there. The south coast – the **Eurobodalla Region** – has plenty of places for nomads to spend time.

You don't have to like wine to love the Hunter Valley, but it certainly helps.

South Australia

A real gem, probably one of the favourite nomadding states. Any of the three peninsulas are fantastic and very popular for nomads. The **Fleurieu Peninsula** including **Victor Harbour**, but in particular a campsite at **Rapid Bay,** is spectacular. From the top of the Fleurieu Peninsula you can get to **Kangaroo Island**. There's lots of camping over there, but it's very expensive to get across on the ferry – a return trip on an RV over 4 metres will set you back at least $200. The **Eyre Peninsula** is beautiful and has lots of free and low-cost camping. **Port Lincoln** and **Coffin Bay** are both beautiful locations and very popular with camping right on the beach in the **Lincoln National Park.** Port Lincoln is ideal for fishing, with Coffin Bay ideal for any oyster lovers. There are some beautiful historic towns close to **Adelaide. Hahndorf** is a Germanic village and extremely popular, and a small place called **Strathalbyn** has a free camp nearby and a nice historic village.

The Flinders Ranges, some 400 kilometres north of Adelaide by road. The colours change constantly depending on how sunlight hits them.

Starting to move up the centre, you go past **Woomera,** which is fascinating for anyone interested in space-related stuff. You cannot ignore the **Flinders Ranges** and the natural ampitheatre of **Wilpena Pound.** There are many campsites and places to stay in the area and it is isolated, but this is what makes it so special. The underground opal-mining town of **Coober Pedy** is another stand out, especially if you want to see something different. It's not for the faint-hearted and it's best to stay in caravan parks for safety, but that said, it is probably one of the more unique places you will see while travelling. **Lake Eyre** is impressive when empty, spectacular when full and **Oodnadatta** is worth a look. Quite a few nomads we have spoken to have done the 'mail run' out there and loved it. There are also lots of great isolated campsites across the **Nullarbor,** for those that love the tranquillity of the outback. The stars out there at night are like nothing you'll see in the cities. And don't forget the **Murray River.** Usually more known for its flow in Victoria, the Murray boasts places such as **Renmark**, **Barmera, Berri** and **Loxton** that are fascinating.

Tasmania

The whole state is worth visiting really. It can be a bit expensive to get over on the ferry, but the trade-off is that once over there, Tassie has lots of free camps. The major cities of **Hobart** and **Launceston** are both very nice – like stepping back in time. In Hobart, all nomads love a trip to **Mount Wellington**, and the **Salamanca Markets** are crowd favourites.

There is, of course, the Sydney to Hobart Yacht Race each year, as well as the massive **Taste of Tasmania food and wine festival**, which is very popular, with some nomads going just for the festival.

Port Arthur. Eerie, peaceful, or both? You be the judge.

There is a place near Hobart called **Richmond** which has some of the best historic buildings on the island, as well as a town called **Ross** further to the north. **Sheffield** and **Raleigh** are beautiful locations, with **Sheffield** knows for its murals – a real hotspot for nomads. **Stanley** and **The Nut** are also very popular for nomads to visit. Across on the west side **Strahan** is an awesome little village and a great place to get fresh crayfish or lobster (whichever you prefer to call them). It also is the access point to the **Franklin River** which offers some amazing river cruises. Then of course there is **Port Arthur** which some say is eerie, but others find peaceful, and full of history.

The Northern Territory

There are just so many places to visit here, starting with the obvious **Uluru, Kata Tjuta** (The Olgas) and **Kings Canyon.** All these are must-see sites and world-renowned for being absolutely spectacular. Many people try to rush these great sites and don't allow enough time to see it all. Don't be one of those people! Uluru, for example, is a 10-kilometre walk right around. You can get lost walking amongst the Olgas, and Kings Canyon is stunning if you can do the rim walk. It is a little steep on the way up, but most nomads give it a go. **The West and East MacDonnell Ranges** are both full of amazing scenery, walks and swimming holes.

Alice Springs itself is an interesting town. In spite of its isolation it still has the necessities and lots of tourist destinations. The **Devils Marbles**, heading north to **Darwin**, is a very popular spot to stop at. In this area there's also **Wycliffe Well** which is noted as being the UFO Capital of Australia. **Daly Waters** has a very isolated pub and quirky pub – the Daly Waters Pub – a mecca for nomads, which is crowded almost every night with great bush entertainment and a steak and barramundi dish they are famous for. **Mataranka** and the **hot springs** is another must-see that most of the nomads love because of the hot springs. You can jump in a natural stream and meander your way downstream for quite a distance. **Katherine** has another character again and **Katherine Gorge** is a very popular spot for nomads to stop off at. **Litchfield National Park** is beautiful and full of gorges and swimming holes, mostly crocodile-free (a bonus!) and an ideal place to cool off at on hot days. Just near there before Darwin is **Berry Springs** – another lot of hot springs, lesser-known but a nice spot. Darwin itself is more like a big country town and very hot and humid.

Unfortunately, one of the big drawbacks with the Northern Territory is that caravan parks are very expensive and there is a lack of free and low-cost camps, especially the closer one gets to

Alice Springs, situated almost in the middle of the continent, and within a comparative stone's throw of some of the more spectacular places Australia has to offer the nomad.

Darwin. One of the most popular things to do in Darwin is the **Mindil Beach Sunset Markets,** and yes, the sunset is spectacular. A trip across to **Kakadu** is fascinating. The **Adelaide River** is full of crocs and plenty of sightseeing things that are croc-related along the way. Kakadu itself is interesting, with lots of Indigenous history, including some ancient Aboriginal artwork. **Cahills Crossing** on the way to **Arnhem Land** is a great place to see yet more crocs and there is a great river cruise that goes a fair way up the river and gives a great insight into the history of the place.

Read this article from FRC about some of the places in the Northern Territory (omitted in this book for those with delicate sensibilities because of the toilet humour):

www.frc.camp/aliceand2teds

Queensland

Ahhh, Queensland! Beautiful one day … Where do we start?

Up north in the Gulf of Carpentaria is **Karumba** – unsealed roads for most of the way, but a very popular destination for nomads. As is **Lawn Hill,** described by many a nomad as an 'oasis in the desert'. Few nomads travel to **Cape York** as you need a 4WD caravan to do it, so most get as far as **Cooktown**, which is a popular RV destination. From there, many leave the coast and venture into outback Queensland and **Dinosaur country. Hughenden, Cloncurry** and **Winton** are popular destinations. Winton has the, **Waltzing Matilda Centre** for dinosaurs and the biannual **Winton Festival** which attracts nomads in droves. **Longreach** has the **Stockman's Hall of Fame** which is another favourite. Many nomads tackle the dirt track through **Boulia** to take a short cut to The Alice and stop off at the annual **Boulia Camel Races** in July along the way. **Birdsville** is another popular destination, as one of the most isolated places in Queensland. The 'world's most isolated music festival', The Big Red Bash, happens west of there in July, which attracts quite a crowd turning the place into a city for a few days, but the nomads probably prefer the **Birdsville Races** in September, over the Bash. Then of course there are the usual tourist spots of the **Gold Coast** and **Sunshine Coast.** Neither are really caravan and camping-friendly but they still have some nice towns in the region to call in on. But many are quite expensive, with most campers giving **Brisbane** a miss.

Left: Gentle paddling at Lawn Hill Gorge, near the North Queensland, Northern Territory border.

The Twelve Apostles

Victoria

Bright, Mount Beauty and **Falls Creek** are cold with snow in winter, beautiful then, but also equally beautiful in the summer months. Anywhere along the **Murray River** is very popular, equally on the New South Wales and Victorian sides. You can follow the river all the way along its course and find a camping spots in some shape or form. **Ballarat** is a popular destination with **Sovereign Hill** especially so. Most campers will avoid **Melbourne**, mainly because caravan parks near there are expensive, but they're still worth a stay if you want to check out the capital city. **The Mornington Peninsula** has lots of great camping along **Port Phillip Bay** and the colourful beach shacks are an enduring attraction. Many then take the ferry across the bay to **Queenscliff** and start their **Great Ocean Road** adventure from there. The Great Ocean Road is spectacular, with the

Sunset, Margaret River, Western Australia

most popular towns being **Lorne** and **Apollo Bay**. **Cape Otway** is also a popular spot for koalas and for the lighthouse. From there, the **Twelve Apostles** are still a crowd favourite, even though there are only about six left now. **Timboon** is a hidden surprise, out in the middle of nowhere, but a foodie haven with lots of nomads loving it.

Western Australia

Starting at the top, most nomads will come in via **Kununurra.** Many will not be aware that they will be stopped at the border and stripped of many food items, especially fruits and including honey. Don't say we didn't warn you! It has a surprising amount of water, so it's also becoming a huge food growing area. Many nomads become fascinated with the farming practices up there. From there, **Lake Argyle** is a must-see: one of the largest man-made lakes in Australia, bigger than Sydney Harbour and home to over 25,000 freshwater crocodiles. The caravan park there has one of the most amazing pools in Australia as it overlooks the lake. The **Kimberleys** and the **Gibb River Road** right through the Top End offers some amazing scenery but, like Cape York in Queensland, the tracks are impassable at certain times of the year. Most will make it to a place called **El Questro** which, at least, is accessible by most 2WD vehicles and caravans. From there, the track across goes past **Halls Creek** and **Fitzroy Crossing,** which have some spectacular gorges, but by this stage, most people have been 'gorged out' from seeing the ones in the NT. For the more adventurous, you can get to the **Wolfe Creek Crater** from here, but many don't like to make the long trip out, probably on account of 'the movie'.

Broome is the next major destination and definitely a must-see if you have come all this way. The **Stairway to the Moon** is one of the most popular attractions. It only happens once a month for a few nights. While there, many will also have a go at the camel rides on **Cable Beach. Cape Leveque** is a popular destination but once again mainly for those nomads that are slightly more adventurous and who have 4WD vans. **Exmouth** and the **Ningaloo Reef** are standout locations and very popular. You can camp right on the beach at Ningaloo and get to the reef, which is only about 20 metres out, as opposed to accessing the Great Barrier Reef, which requires larger boats and is quite a distance offshore. There is also the opportunity to swim with the whale sharks from here at certain times of the year. **Coral Bay** is another stand out location – lots of … well … coral, as well as fish and sea life to see with just a short swim from shore.

Carnarvon remains another popular spot for nomads to stop off, recharge and restock because, like Kununurra, it's a popular area for growing fruit and vegetables. The bananas grown in the region are possibly the best in Australia. Take note also of **Marble Bar,** a fascinating mining area if you like that sort of thing, and where the ground is streaked with marble effects. The locale is extremely hot, one of the hottest places in Australia, so it's best to go in winter months. There's also **Karijini National Park** and **The Bungle Bungles.** You can't drive caravans into them and the road is extremely corrugated, but they are one of the most amazing landforms people will see in the outback. **Monkey Mia** is isolated, but a standout if you want to interact with dolphins. There's not much there other than the resort and campground, but it's a good place to meet up with fellow nomads. **Kalbarri National Park** is a popular spot and **The Pinnacles** are high on the list of places to see.

Many nomads from the eastern states are fascinated with **Perth** and **Fremantle.** There's quite a bit to see and do in both places, but it's best to stay in caravan parks on the outer edges. South of Perth the beaches are spectacular, especially at **Busselton,** but be warned, from here on south caravan parks are quite expensive. The entire **Margaret River** is extremely popular. The area consists of quite a few scattered towns and villages along the coastline. **Cowaramup** is unusual and has fun painted cows all around town. There are wineries, cafes and galleries galore. One of the most visited locations in Western Australia is **Esperance** as it has one of the most magnificent beaches in Australia. And of course, **Kalgoorlie** is there for those wanting to check out the gold mines. **Wave Rock** is a famous, naturally formed rock in the shape of a wave – as the name implies. From **Norseman** people cross over the **Nullarbor** and one of the most popular attractions here is the nine-hole golf course – spread over hundreds of kilometres. Halfway to the border with South Australia is **Madura**, at its top, **Madura Pass.** You can camp there for the night, high up on a ridge with spectacular views over to the Great Australian Bight. It almost looks like the savannah lands of Africa.

A Year on the Road: Calendar of Events

Australia, being the continent-size country that it is, has a lot going on all the time.

FRC publishes newsletters regularly, containing lists of upcoming events including caravan shows, featured events and festivals that might be particularly suited to campers and nomads. So you can plan your trip to be at the right place at the right time. The newsletters are free to subscribe to and all available at: **www.frc.camp/enews**

See also **www.thegreynomads.com.au/events**

We also recommend making the local Visitor Information Centre your first stop whenever you arrive anywhere, just in case you come at a time that something that you're interested in might be happening.

The list below is just to give you a teensy-weensy taste of what's on offer throughout the country, throughout the year.

JANUARY

NSW; Country Music Festival, Tamworth – **www.tcmf.com.au**
SA; Port Lincoln Tunarama Festival, Port Lincoln Foreshore – **www.tunarama.net**

FEBRUARY

TAS; Festivale, Launceston (starts late January) – **www.festivale.com.au**
TAS; Australian Wooden Boat Festival, Hobart – **www.australianwoodenboatfestival.com.au**
VIC; Riverboats Music Festival, Echuca-Moama – **www.riverboatsmusic.com.au**

MARCH

VIC; Moomba Festival, Melbourne – **www.moomba.melbourne.vic.gov.au**

APRIL

NSW; Australian Celtic Festival, Glen Innes –
www.australiancelticfestival.com/about
NSW; Taste Tamworth Festival, Tamworth –
**www.destinationtamworth.com.au/Events/Food---
Culture/taste-tamworth-festival**
QLD; Roma's Easter in the Country, Roma –
www.easterinthecountryroma.com.au

MAY

VIC; Melbourne's Good Beer Week –
www.goodbeerweek.com.au

JUNE

NSW; Winter Magic Festival, Katoomba –
www.wintermagic.com.au

JULY

NT; Katherine and District Show, Katherine –
www.katherineshow.org.au
QLD;Cooktown Festival, Cooktown –
www.cooktown2020.com (we imagine that the website changes
its number every year)

AUGUST

QLD; Mount Isa Rodeo, Mount Isa – **www.isarodeo.com.au**

SEPTEMBER

ACT; Floriade, Canberra – **www.floriadeaustralia.com**

OCTOBER

NSW; Grafton Jacaranda Festival, Grafton –
www.jacarandafestival.com
WA; Margaret River Gourmet Escape –
www.gourmetescape.com.au

NOVEMBER

SA; Edinburgh Air Show, Edinburgh, Adelaide –
www.airforce.gov.au/exercises/edinburghairshow2020
(we imagine that the website changes its number every year) SA –
A Day at the Burgh, Edithburgh – **www.edithburgh.org.au**
WA; Fremantle Craft Beer Festival, Fremantle –
www. fremantle.beerfestivals.com.au

DECEMBER

TAS; Rolex Sydney-Hobart Yacht Race, Hobart –
www.rolexsydneyhobart.com
TAS; Taste of Tasmania, Hobart –
www.thetasteoftasmania.com.au

Some Final Thoughts

Nomadding is a huge subject. It is, after all, a whole life change that requires a whole new knowledge base and skillset. This book could easily be ten times bigger than it is, but do you really need to carry around a doorstop? Haven't we told you time and time again about the virtues of travelling light? If we've given you a good head start on your journey and pointed you in the right direction to make fully informed choices, then we've done our job. And if you've already taken the step and we've shown you a thing or two, then we've done our job even better!

Feel free to get back to us with feedback.

We'd love to know what we could do better for future editions of *The Grey Nomad's Ultimate Guide to Australia*.

Contact us at:
info@fullrangecamping.com.au
But for now we wish you the very best on your grand adventure.

Appendix One: Emergencies

The nationwide emergency telephone number is **000.**

In an emergency, it might be difficult to maintain your presence of mind, but the calmer you are and the more information that you can give, the more the emergency services can help you. Staff at the **000** call centre are trained to be as helpful as possible in getting what they need from you so put your trust in them.

Decide whether you want ambulance, fire brigade, police, or all three. This is the first question that they will ask you and they will prioritise based on what you tell them.

If you're calling from a landline, they'll be able to trace the call (in most cases) and they'll know where you're calling from. If you're calling from a mobile phone or satellite phone they can sometimes trace your call but if you can do your best to give them an idea of your location. You might be asked what 'state' you're in. This is a necessary question since street names and even town names are repeated in many states so they don't want to send your help to an address in Coogee New South Wales if you happen to be in Coogee Western Australia. If you can, provide a street number, street name, nearest cross street and inform them if you're near a significant landmark.

Special Notes for Ambulance

State the nature of emergency to the best of your ability.

- How many people are in distress?
- Age of distressed parties?
- Gender?
- Conscious or Unconscious?
- Breathing or Not Breathing?

Do not hang up until the operator tells you to. You might need to stay on the line until help arrives in order to listen to advice, instructions or simply to maintain the integrity of the connection for a trace.

Appendix Two: Australia's Climatic Zones

Australia is so big that it has eight climate zones. It pays to know which one you're in so that you can be prepared for how to arrange your clothing and shelter. The major differences between the climates are the temperatures in summer and winter, as well as whether it's the summer or the winter that favours rainfall or if there's ever much rain in the first place. The zones are:

Climate Zone 1: summer high humidity, warm winter. Includes equatorial and tropical zones, with rainforest that are persistently wet or have monsoonal rains and savannahs.

Climate Zone 2: summer, mild winter. Subtropical but varying from areas with no dry season to dry seasons in either the summer or the winter.

Climate Zone 3: summer hot and dry, warm winter. From persistently dry to seasonally dry deserts and some persistently or seasonally dry grasslands

Climate Zone 4: Summer hot and dry, cool winter. Dominated by desert and persistently to seasonally dry grasslands.

Climate Zone 5: warm temperate. Mostly warm grasslands with some subtropical areas with distinctly dry summers.

Climate Zone 6: mild temperate regions with either no dry season or seasonally dry summers or winters.

Climate Zone 7: cool temperate. Mild summers and cool, wet winters.

Climate Zone 8: alpine. Mild moderately dry summers and cold, snowy winters.

Detailed Australia-Wide Climate Zone Map, State and Metropolitan Maps

www.abcb.gov.au/Resources/Tools-Calculators/Climate-Zone-Map-Australia-Wide

www.bom.gov.au/climate/how/newproducts/images/zones.shtml

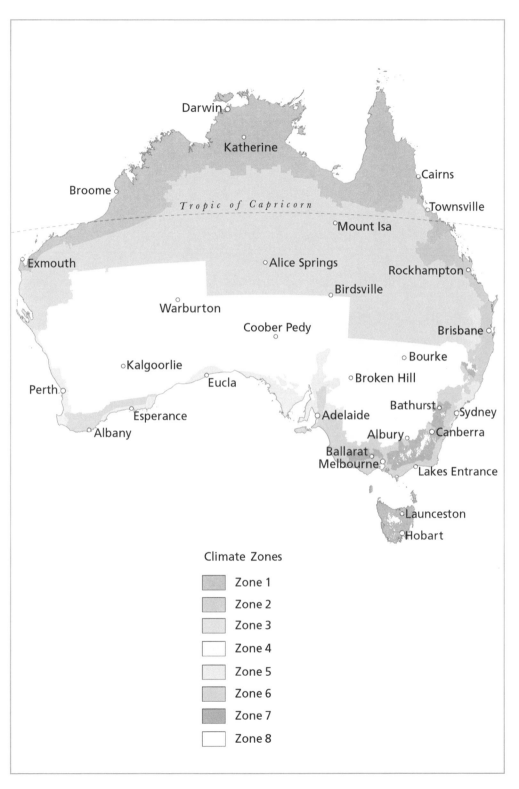

Darwin

Katherine

Cairns

Broome

Tropic of Capricorn

Townsville

Mount Isa

Exmouth

Alice Springs

Rockhampton

Birdsville

Warburton

Coober Pedy

Brisbane

Kalgoorlie

Bourke

Eucla

Broken Hill

Perth

Bathurst

Sydney

Esperance

Adelaide

Albury

Canberra

Albany

Ballarat
Melbourne

Lakes Entrance

Launceston

Hobart

Climate Zones

Zone 1

Zone 2

Zone 3

Zone 4

Zone 5

Zone 6

Zone 7

Zone 8

Appendix Three: Checklists

Preparing for the trip

- Read this book
- Join FRC

The RV (caravan, motorhome, campervan or trailer)

List of what to do before a long trip

- Undergo a full service of all the vehicles you'll be taking with you
- Check and test all fire safety equipment including
  - Fire blankets
  - Fire alarms
  - Carbon monoxide alarms

List of what to pack and take

Sanitary and cleaning items:

- Dustpan and broom
- Dishwashing essentials
- Detergent
- Tubs or bucket (or strucket)
- Soap
- Towels
- Washers and wash cloths etc.
- Face netting to protect you from sand-flies and midges
- Mini vacuum, 12V or otherwise
- Bin and bin liners
- Laundry items
- Clothes basket or bag
- Detergents
- Pegs and peg bag
- Mini clothesline or hanging device

RV items:
- Fuses
- Jack
- Wheel brace
- Wheel chocks
- Hitch locks or wheel clamps

Camping and outdoor items:
- Chairs, folding
- Camping table
- Door mats
- Annex mat
- Lighting, LED
- Torches
- Camp oven
- Heatproof gloves
- Fire starters
- Torches
- Power leads (both 10 amp and 15 amp)
- Axe
- Hand saw or small 18 V chainsaw

Entertainment:
- Games and cards
- Books or reading material
- Camera
- Phone chargers
- Fishing gear
- Sporting goods

Kitchen Items:
- Toaster
- Kettle
- Crockery
- Utensils – the most useful of which will be a cast-iron skillet and that kettle

Tools:

- Hammer
- Spanners and sockets
- Screwdrivers
- Pliers, cutters, multigrips
- Cordless drill and bits
- Puncture repairs
- 12 V pump (inflator)
- Cable ties
- Silicon
- Glue
- Spare nuts, bolts and screws

Hitching up check list

- Check couplings
- Double-check couplings
- Safety chains – condition; secured
- Stabiliser bars – fitted; secured
- Electrical wiring from car to van/trailer
- Lights – breaks; indicators; headlights; driving lights
- Breakaway cables if required
- Mirrors – attached; checked
- Tyres – tread; pressures; spare wheel; nuts
- Batteries – car; house batteries
- Jockey wheel
- Water tanks – leaks; full/empty
- Toilets – empty; treatments
- Gas bottles – full; turned off; secured
- Disconnect from 240 mains
- Fridge ventilation
- Payload equal
- Baton down the hatches
- Securer all items in the van
- Doors closed and secured

Arriving at Destination

Check the site for:

Suitability

   Dampness – is it too boggy?

   Escape routes – can you get out easily if you need to?

Site Condition

- Is it clean?
- Is it safe?
- Is it clear?
- Sticks and rocks

Proximity to neighbouring vans

Access to (if needed)

- Power
- Water
- Toilets

Unhitch

Level

Secure

Connect to (if required)

- Power
- Water
- Waste (grey water)

Unpack:

- Internal items
- Outdoor items – camp chairs; tables; wine and snacks

Other options if required:

- Set up satellite TV
- Set up TV reception

Appendix Four: Further Reading, Watching and Listening

Customising, Fitting Out and Converting an RV

These are just a few of the scores of videos out there. You could spend hours watching these things and getting ideas.

www.youtube.com/watch?v=5h-B_t5xZSY
www.youtube.com/watch?v=wapg3iJE9Es
www.youtube.com/watch?v=ko-F0Ma4i-w
www.youtube.com/watch?v=dUKc1TGS-bU

Depreciation

www.godownsize.com/rv-depreciation-guide

The Future of Nomadism

www.abc.net.au/news/2018-12-10/how-the-grey-nomad-lifestyle-may-change/10599340
www.thehub.nrma.com.au/drive/grey-nomad-phenomenon

Getting Educated, Staying Educated

www.training.nsw.gov.au/ace/index.html

Money Matters
www.goseeaustralia.com.au/blog/ways-to-save-money-full-time-nomad-australia

And while we're on the subject, here are the answers to the financial literacy question on page 46:

1. $102
2. No. You'd have only $99. Interest gives you $1. Inflation eats up $2.

3. False. Spreading your investments spreads the risk too.
4. Yes. The bigger the potential risk the bigger the potential returns and vice versa.
5. You'd have the same buying power, only the numbers would get bigger.

On the Road

www.thegreynomads.activeboard.com/t64658586/ road-train-etiquette

YouTube Channels
'Carolyn's RV Life'
'CheapRVliving' – **www.cheaprvliving.com**
'FRC's YouTube Channel' – **www.frc.camp/frcyoutube**
'Matt's RV Reviews' – very useful for tips
'RV Odd Couple' – **www.rvoddcouple.com**
'RV Lifestyle'
'RV Love' – **www.rvlife.com**
'RV Travel Newsletter'
'RV Wingman'

Transitioning Too Fast – Entry and Exit Strategies
www.opuscamper.com.au/four-sleeper-camper
www.podtrailer.com.au

Appendix Five: Your Guide to the FRC app

The FRC app is one of the most useful tools out there for campers and nomads.

Firstly, there is the free website for anyone to use:

www.fullrangecamping.com.au

And here are the tutorial videos to show you how to use it, particularly the directory to find campsites: **www.frc.camp/tutorials**

Here are all the benefits of being a Premium Member:

www.frc.camp/premium

From here, you can find out more about the features of the FRC app for premium members. Once you log in as a Premium Member, you'll be on the Welcome Premium Members page. On the side menu you'll see app Video Tutorials. Click there to continue so that you can watch more than twenty easy-to-understand videos that will show you the full power of the app and all that it can do for you.

Appendix Six: FRC Premium Benefits

Throughout this guidebook we've made mention of the various benefits available to Premium Members of FRC. As a quick and ready reference, here's a full list of those benefits:

Access to The Directory: the real-time updated directory of over 10,000 sites, including free camps, campgrounds and caravan parks as well as relevant recreational-vehicle-related businesses throughout Australia. Available online and as an app that you can use on your smart phone or tablet and that works whether you are online or offline.

The Directory search engine allows you to search for:

- Information centres
- Free camps, rest areas, campgrounds and caravan parks
- House sitting and help-out opportunities
- Dump points
- Accommodation
- Camping accessories
- Entertainment
- Food and drinks, groceries and markets
- Medical assistance and personal health

In addition, you can search for the availability of:

- Suitable, not suitable, permitted or not permitted for tents, camper trailers, caravans, campervans and motor homes, big rig access or fully self-contained camping vehicles only
- Toilets, showers, laundry, drinkable and non-drinkable water
- 4WD access, dry weather access and locations shared with trucks
- Pets permitted or not permitted
- Disabled facilities
- Internet access, mobile phone reception, emergency phones
- Power or generators permitted or not
- Fires permitted or not

- Rubbish bins and dump points
- On-site accommodation, ensuites, games rooms
- Kiosk, restaurant, camp kitchen or nearby pubs
- Children's playgrounds, BBQs, picnic tables, shelter or shade
- Showgrounds, swimming and boat ramps
- National parks and forestry and national park fees, views
- Time limits at site

Each directory listing includes a map displaying site addresses and locations, with a link to Google or Apple Maps that lists the websites of the sites, telephone number, opening hours and the option of getting directions there from your current location, or from any location within Australia.

Typical available information also includes a brief description of camps, sites and businesses, email addresses, website addresses and pricing. Members also have the option of looking at ratings and comments from other members or to leave a review themselves.

There is also a fully integrated weather app that gives a weather forecast at each campsite for a seven-day period. It includes a rain radar, wind warnings, tide and sunset times and much more.

Other benefits of FRC Premium Membership include:

- A complimentary six-month membership to the Kiu Parks Group of caravan parks, which includes 10 per cent off at over 80 parks throughout Australia.
- Discounts of up to 30 per cent at participating independent caravan parks and campgrounds.
  - Discounts and special offers at national outlets such as:
  - 5–10 per cent off at participating IGA stores
  - 10 per cent off at Battery World outlets
  - 20 per cent off at participating Tint a Car stores
  - Wholesale pricing in the FRC Shop with savings of up to 50 per cent off selected products.
- Access to a specialised Caravan and Motorhome Insurance Policy that provides prestige cover to members.

A Special Offer for Buyers of *The Grey Nomad's Ultimate Guide to Australia*

FRC would like to offer an exclusive deal, only available to purchasers of *The Grey Nomad's Ultimate Guide to Australia.*

This offer comprises a one-year PREMIUM Membership to FRC with all the benefits listed in Appendix 6. Full Range Premium Membership normally costs $44.95, but for purchasers of *The Grey Nomad's Ultimate Guide to Australia* you can join up and secure your membership at a discount of over 30 per cent.

It's yours for only $29.95.

To take advantage of this special offer simply go to FRC's secure website: **frc.camp/greyoffer.** Fill in all the appropriate information and quote the discount code: **FRCGREY**

First published in 2020 by New Holland Publishers
This edition published by New Holland Publishers 2021
Sydney • Auckland

Level 1, 178 Fox Valley Road, Wahroonga 2076, Australia
5/39 Woodside Ave, Northcote, Auckland 0627, New Zealand
newhollandpublishers.com

A record of this book is held at the National Library of Australia.

ISBN 9781760792039

Group Managing Director: Fiona Schultz
Publisher: Fiona Schultz
Project Editor: Liz Hardy
Designer: Yolanda La Gorcé
Production Director: Arlene Gippert

Printed in China

10 9 8 7 6 5 4

Keep up with New Holland Publishers:

 NewHollandPublishers

 @newhollandpublishers